BOSTON
PUBLIC
LIBRARY

Past, Space, and Self

John Campbell

A Bradford Book
The MIT Press
Cambridge, Massachusetts
London, England

© 1994 Massachusetts Institute of Technology

This book was set in Sabon by The Maple-Vail Book Manufacturing Group and was printed and bound in the United States of America.

First printing.

Library of Congress Cataloging-in-Publication Data

Campbell, John, 1956–
    Past, space, and self / John Campbell.
        p.   cm. — (Representation and mind)
    "A Bradford book."
    Includes bibliographical references and index.
    ISBN 0-262-03215-5
    1. Space and time. 2. Mental representation. 3. Schemas (Psychology) 4. Egoism. I. Title. II. Series.
BF467.C35   1944
153.7—dc20   93-14038
                                                     CIP

For Sarah

Contents

Preface

This book began ten years ago with a conviction that an understanding of the first person has a foundational place in the theory of meaning and metaphysics. It has taken a long time to reach an articulation of the idea. In April 1990, I visited the project on Spatial Representation at King's College, Cambridge, and worked up the basis for this material. I owe an immense amount especially to Naomi Eilan for her sense of direction and uncompromising support, as well as to the other members of the project: Bill Brewer, Tony Marcel, Roz McCarthy, and Ian McLaren. Through the project, I met John O'Keefe, whose combination of zest and deep learning made it a pleasure to work on space.

What delayed me more than anything else was my acceptance of the conventional view that there is a dichotomy between an understanding of the first person as a piece of language governed by the rule that any token of 'I' refers to whoever produced it, on which it has nothing to do with self-consciousness, and an understanding of it as a kind of quasi-perceptual demonstrative meaning something like 'this person', on which it does express self-consciousness. Long discussions with Philippa Foot, beginning in 1988, were what forced me to abandon that view, and I benefited a great deal also from discussions on the topic with Quassim Cassam and Timothy Williamson.

Over the years I have learned much from Charles Travis, whose strictures on context dependence I have tried to observe. Philosophers vary in how much they learn from those around them. I have always been aware of learning a great deal. In particular, I must thank Justin Broackes, David Charles, Jonathan Glover, Carsten Hansen, Susan Hurley, Gavin Lawrence, Michael Luntley, Penelope Mackie, Nick Rawlins, and Joanna Woodall, as well as the MIT Press and its reviewers. In 1991, I visited the Australian National University in Canberra and while there prepared the penultimate version of this material. The warmth of Philip Pettit and Eileen McNally made it a very pleasant trip. I completed this version in perfect surroundings, thanks to the generosity of Carsten and Georg Hansen.

I have kept my principal debt till last. Through discussion and through his books, Michael Dummett has affected my conception of what philosophy is and the depth and energy with which it is possible to pursue it.

Past, Space, and Self

Introduction

In Somerset Maugham's *Of Human Bondage* the hero is given a densely patterned Persian carpet and assured that in its design lies the solution to the problem of meaning. Naturally, he examines the carpet closely, searching for encrypted messages or hidden pictures. Eventually it dawns on him that the point is not any individual detail but the whole design. One has to weave all the details of one's life into a meaningful pattern. This book is about one of the rudimentary prerequisites of achieving that sense of pattern: self-consciousness. Self-consciousness involves at least the capacity to think in terms of the story of one's past life. It is also a prerequisite of ordinary social interaction. Indeed, one of the most basic kinds of social interaction, from a developmental point of view, is the sharing of memories between parent and child. This kind of social bonding seems to be part of what explains the evolutionary benefit, the selection value, of autobiographical memory.

Self-consciousness, as I describe it, is not just a matter of thinking of oneself as temporally extended, so that one has a sequence of states one after the other. It involves grasping one's own causal structure. There are two dimensions to this grasp of causal structure. There is grasp of the idea that one's later states causally depend, in part, on one's earlier states: when one interacts with one's surroundings, what happens is the joint upshot of the character of the things around one and the way one is oneself. The other dimension in grasp of one's own causal structure is the idea that one can function as a common cause of various correlated events around one. Schematically, one topic that will concern us is the relation between knowledge of one's physical characteristics and knowledge of one's psychological characteristics in grasping one's causal structure.

The project of the book is to determine the relation between, on the one hand, grasp of the first person, which is the most immediate expression of self-consciousness, and, on the other, the ability to think about the spatial layout of the environment and one's place in it and the ability to think about time as extending forward and backward, the ability to orient oneself in a temporal frame of reference.

What is the plan of the book? I begin by describing the spatiotemporal framework presupposed by conceiving of oneself as causally structured in two dimensions. There is a kind of objectivity possible in spatial thinking that has to do with the possibility of assigning causal significance to spatial properties and relations at a reflective level removed from the immediate practical demands of interaction with one's surroundings. This kind of reflective or objective spatial thinking turns out to be demanded by thought about the past, about the history of oneself and one's surroundings. These first two chapters describe the basic spatiotemporal framework that we use. I then turn to the first person to try to determine how understanding it depends on grasp of that framework. I describe the sense of the first person and what it means to say that there is such a thing. I consider the relation of an understanding of the first person to grasp of the two dimensions of one's causal structure and also consider its connection with self-knowledge and ordinary social interaction. Some have held, contrary to the whole thrust of this book, that the concept of the self is in fact not fundamental in our thinking and that it is better dispensed with altogether. So I look at the bases of this reductionist view. Then I draw things together and set out the way in which grasp of one's causal structure demands use of the spatiotemporal framework.

In describing these basic modes of thought about oneself and one's world, I am describing a cluster of conceptual abilities fundamental to ordinary thinking. Indeed, they define what conceptual thinking is: I argue that the ability to engage in these basic patterns of thought is what sets apart a conceptual thinker from an animal capable only of more primitive types of representation or simply of different types of representation. Possession of this core set of abilities defines possession of concepts. Throughout the book it would have been possible to use a systematic notation to differentiate human thinking from the representational methods used by other animals. I have not done this, partly because it is always obvious whether or not I am talking about human thinking, so there is no important ambiguity, and partly because one main aim of this book is to earn the right to that distinction, so it would have been doctrinaire simply to lay down from the outset how the distinction is to be applied. I hope the reader who already believes in a firm distinction between human conceptual thinking and other types of representation will not be unduly depressed by the fact that the distinction is not presupposed in what follows; ultimately, the point is to provide a foundation for the distinction.

The aim of this book is to show that a realist view of the past is presupposed in the exercise of these basic conceptual abilities, the conceptual skills constitutive of self-consciousness. This line of argument gives a different place to self-consciousness in philosophy from that traditionally given to it. The classical reason for giving a central place to self-consciousness was to respond to skepticism: self-consciousness seemed to be a foundational point from which one might begin. The resulting notion of self-consciousness, restricted to aspects of the self about which one could not be wrong, bears little relation to self-consciousness as an everyday phenomenon and is of little interest outside that particular epistemological debate. I am proposing a different role for self-consciousness. It can be viewed as setting certain fundamental norms of thought. It is the basis of the demand for causal structure in one's conceptual organization, causal structure that is distinctive of possession of concepts. And it demands a realist view of the past.

The fact that a realist view of the past is demanded by self-consciousness does not of itself show that realism about the past is correct. This would involve a kind of background idealism: supposing that the form of the world is somehow an artifact of the demands of self-consciousness. But it has to be acknowledged that very general facts about the world can be discovered by other means. For example, perhaps quantum mechanics will ultimately be seen to have implications for our understanding of the past. Perhaps quantum mechanics will even show that the kind of reflective understanding of our place in the world that I describe in this book cannot in the end be achieved. But that would not show that we should simply set aside realism about the past and self-consciousness. Rather, a profound conflict would have been generated. Even though there is no guarantee that the demands of self-consciousness will be met by the world, whether to be self-conscious is in practice not a matter about which we have any choice. For as I began by remarking, self-consciousness is a precondition of ordinary social interaction. And it is needed if one is to find any kind of narrative meaning in life.

1

Frames of Reference

1.1 The Distinction

There is a distinction that philosophers and psychologists have tried to draw between different ways of thinking about space, about particular spatial regions. It is sometimes called, and I will call it, the distinction between *absolute* and *egocentric* space. But it is not a distinction between different types of regions. It is a difference between ways of representing, or thinking about, a particular region. The distinction is at best very indirectly related to the classifications physicists make of theories of space-time as relativistic or absolute. For that reason the word 'absolute' is unfortunate. But it is what the literature uses, and I hope the reader will be able to set these echoes aside.

Intuitively, the distinction is between thinking about space as a participant, as someone plunged into its center, as someone with things to do in that space, on the one hand, and, on the other hand, thinking about the space as a disengaged theorist. Any animal that has the relations between perception and behavior needed to direct action at particular places, to reach for things it can see, must be capable of this egocentric spatial thinking. But the more detached absolute conception is not so easily available. The distinction is between the way of thinking of the space one is in that one uses when sitting at a dinner table, moving and acting in that space, and the way of thinking of the space used subsequently by the detective who tries to reconstruct the scene and to establish who did what. It is the distinction between thinking about the space from a particular point of view, as a subject at the center of one's world, and thinking about the space independently of any particular viewpoint on it, in an impersonal or absolute way.

The idea of absolute space sometimes appears in discussions of self-consciousness. When self-consciousness is conceived in this way, it can seem dizzying. What it demands is that one should build up a synoptic picture of the world, one that wholly abstracts from one's own place in the throng, and then somehow identify one of the people so pictured as oneself. What is dizzying is the kind of complete objectivity, the degree of abstraction from one's own busy concerns, that is required. A first interpretation is that what is wanted is a kind of top-down view, so that we think in terms of a kind of aerial photograph, and then one has to identify oneself as one of the people shown in the photo. But that would not be enough, for it would only give the viewpoint of the photographer, and we need a picture of the world that is objective, in that it is not from any viewpoint at all. It is a picture not drawn from any perspective. A natural reaction to this demand is to move the photographer further away from the earth, but of course no finite amount of movement will be enough. And once he is at an infinite distance, what will he be able to photograph? What would you expect to be able to discern from nowhere?

One reaction to the vertigo here would be to say that we do not need any kind of objective conception in order to be self-conscious. Immersed, as we are, in the thick of things, we have no need or use for such a conception in our everyday lives, whereas self-consciousness is commonplace. So an objective conception is not demanded by self-consciousness. But this reaction leaves us in the dark about what self-consciousness might be. The real problem is not the notion of an objective conception as such but the way of interpreting the spatial imagery that leads to the dizziness just described. Self-consciousness does demand a kind of objectivity and does use a conception of absolute space. But to understand the notion of objectivity involved, what we have to look at is our ordinary thinking about time. What matters is the way we think about the historical order of events that have happened and are going to happen and about our own temporal location in that order—the span of our lives within it and where things stand now. We will see that this really does involve a kind of objectivity and does use a conception of absolute space, and it certainly matters in ordinary life.

It is part of the distinction between absolute and egocentric space that the absolute conception should not be somehow reducible to, or definable in terms of, the egocentric spatial thinking used in perception and action. For this reason, the distinction has characteristically been rejected by philosophers of an empiricist or pragmatist bent, who think that all ways of representing space must be explicable in terms of their connections with perception and action, in terms of their relations to egocentric space. In this chapter we will first look more critically at the question of how to characterise an egocentric frame of reference. We will then look at John O'Keefe's specific description of an absolute frame of reference and determine how well it stands up to empiricist-pragmatist criticism. We will see that a notion of absolute space can ultimately be sustained and that it is used in our ordinary thinking about time. One question we will consider is whether, in constructing such an absolute or objective frame of reference, physical objects play any role; they certainly do not seem to be needed in constructing an egocentric frame.

1.2   Egocentric Frames

Let us begin, then, with egocentric spatial thinking. The frame of reference that we use to identify places in directing our actions, in deciding where to move to, is an egocentric frame. On the face of it, an egocentric frame is a body-centered frame or one centered on a part of the body. The developmental psychologists Herbert Pick and Jeffrey Lockman (1981) put the idea as follows. They define a *frame of reference* to be "a locus or set of loci with respect to which spatial position is defined." *Egocentric* frames of reference then are those that "define spatial positions in relation to loci on the body." They are contrasted with *allocentric* frames of reference, "which simply means that the positions defining loci are external to the person in question" (1981, 40). This definition seems indeed to give a reductive account of the notion of an egocentric frame, defining it in terms of notions that genuinely seem to be more fundamental than it.

It is worth reflecting on the general form of the definition. In trying to say what is characteristic of an egocentric frame of reference, I am not dealing with a problem in pure mathematics. It is not, for example, on a level with the question of whether a frame of reference uses polar or Cartesian coordinates. In purely formal terms, the best we could do would be to say that it must be possible, using an egocentric frame, to specify spatial relations to a single privileged point, but that would not separate an egocentric frame from one centered on the sun, for example. We have to say something about the physical significance of the origin of the frame: we want to say,

for example, that it must be centered on the subject. This notion of the subject is not a purely formal notion of pure mathematics. But saying where the frame is centered is only one way
of giving physical significance to the formal notions. An alternative would be to consider the physical significance of the axes
of the frame of reference and to take them as fundamental. An
egocentric frame would then be one whose axes had a particular kind of physical significance. It would then be a substantive
thesis, rather than a definition, that egocentric frames are invariably centered on the body, or a part of the body. And it
would be quite wrong, on that approach, to suppose that in
using an egocentric frame, one must be identifying places by
their relations to a body already identified.

The definition of an egocentric frame as a body-centered
frame takes for granted the general notion of an object-centered frame of reference, and it says that the egocentric frames
are a particular class of object-centered frame, namely, those
centered on the body or a part of the body. The general notion
of an object-centered frame is certainly legitimate. Consider an
object such as a table or a bus. We can think of the internal
spatial relations between its parts. We can use this system of
internal spatial relations to identify points within the object.
There may be natural axes that the object has. For example,
given a pillar-box, we could define a set of axes by reference to
its long axis, its line of sight as through the slot, and its coronal
plane as through which the door moves when it is opened. So
far what we have is a way of identifying points internal to the
object. But the system of spatial relations that I have set up
between the parts of the thing can be further used to identify
points external to it. We could, for instance, identify a coconut
on a palm tree as lying on a line through the bottom of one leg
of a table and the top of another, and a hundred yards distant

in the direction going from bottom to top. This way of identifying places need not be used only with inanimate objects as its basis. One could equally well take the internal spatial relations between the parts of a horse, or its natural axes, and use them to give fully allocentric identifications of the places around it. One could do the same with a human body; one could do the same with what is in fact one's own body. And then, by Pick and Lockman's definition, what we have is an egocentric frame. Evidently, there is a finer distinction that we want to make here. For it is not as if we can assume extensionality: not just any way of thinking of the subject will do. The notion of egocentric space is a psychological notion; the reason we want it is to explain why the infant, for example, turns one way rather than another. In particular, perceptual knowledge of the body will not do. Merely seeing one's own body in a mirror, for example, and using it to set up a system of axes will not provide one with an egocentric frame.

The obvious proposal is that the subject has to be using direct, nonobservational knowledge of his own body constituted by his possession of a body image. In one use of the phrase 'the body image', it has to be thought of as referring to a relatively long-term picture of one's own physical dimensions. So someone's body image might be changed as a result of their having a skin graft or the loss of a limb or simply by growing up. In this use of the term, one's body image provides one with a general sense of what kinds of movement are possible for one. It assigns a particular structure to a creature that underlies its possibilities of movement. We cannot directly use this structure to set up a system of axes: it assigns no particular shape to the body. What we need is rather what O'Shaughnessy calls the "here and now" body image, which "is given by the description or drawing or model one would assemble in order to say how the body seems to one *at a certain instant*. For example: torso straight, right cylindrical arm stretched out from body, crooked at right angles, etc." (1980, 241). If a person has such a body image, he can plot the spatial relations between the various parts of his body and use them to construct a body-centered set of axes that will indeed be the egocentric axes. This proposal relies on a direct relation between the subject's body image and his ability to act. We have to think of the body image as giving the subject a practical grasp of the ways in which it is possible to act, the possibilities of movement open to him. Of course, there must be some relation between these two conceptions of a body image. The immediate problem, though, is to understand why this shift, from outer perception of the body, such as seeing it in a mirror, to inner perception, as provided by a short-term body image, should be thought to achieve anything. After all, as we saw, simply managing to use the spatial relations between the parts of the body to set up a system of axes does not in general secure one an egocentric frame. Why should we think that an egocentric frame is guaranteed if one relies on the spatial relations between the parts of the body given in inner perception? The point here is that there is in general no direct connection between the mere use of an arbitrarily chosen body to set up coordinate axes and the subject's capacity for directed spatial action. What the present proposal relies on is a direct relation between a subject's short-term body image and his ability to act. We have to think of the short-term body image as giving the subject a practical grasp of the ways in which he can act, the possibilities of movement open to him. The reason this seems promising is that the short-term body image has direct connections with action of the type possessed by the egocentric axes. The proposal is that we can view the direct connection between action and egocentric space as a product of the direct connection between action and the short-term body image. But now we have to ask how the body image has this direct connection with action. And we immediately face a dilemma. For how are the spatial relations between the parts of the body given in the body image? One possibility is that they are given in egocentric terms: one foot is represented as to the right of another, below the rest of the body, and so on. But then it can hardly be held that the subject uses the natural axes of his body to set up the egocentric axes; rather, he already has to use the egocentric frame to grasp the spatial relations between the parts of his body. Alternatively, suppose that the spatial relations between the parts of one's body are given in nonegocentric terms. Then there is no prospect of using the axes of one's body to set up an egocentric frame; one is in no better a position to do this with respect to the body of which one has inner perception than one would be with respect to a body of which one has outer perception. In both cases the problem is the same. One's grasp of egocentric spatial axes, with their immediate connections to moving and acting, cannot be generated from a grasp of spatial relations that are nonegocentrically given. Grasp of egocentric spatial axes must be taken as primitive.

This means that a certain kind of reductive ambition for the definition of an egocentric frame as a body-centered frame has to be abandoned. We cannot view this definition as explaining the notion of egocentricity in more fundamental terms. We cannot see it as defining egocentricity in terms of the generic notion of an object-centered frame of reference plus the notion of a body-centered frame. For when we inquire into the needed notion of body-centeredness, it turns out that it already appeals to the notion of the body as given in the body image, with its spatial relations given egocentrically. In particular, then, we cannot take the body image to be more fundamental than the egocentric axes; we cannot derive them from it. The egocentric axes have to be taken as primitive, relative to the body image.

It might be asked whether the body image is not at any rate coordinate with the egocentric axes, so that they have to be taken as equally fundamental for spatial action. But while some egocentric reference frame is evidently essential if we are to have spatial action—otherwise the action could not be re-garded as spatial at all—it does not seem that a subject needs to have a body image to be capable of egocentric spatial action, action we would want to explain by appealing to his possession of an egocentric frame of reference. Coordination and direction of spatial action may be achieved by purely distal specifications of the locations that are the endpoints of the actions, without the subject's having a single central body image at all (Scott Kelso 1982). If a body image is superimposed on the subject's egocentric axes, this is in addition to the requirements for him to be thinking about places egocentrically. So when the subject is identifying places egocentrically, he cannot be thought of as doing so by first identifying a physical thing, himself, through a body image and then identifying places by their relation to his body. Rather, his capacity to use the egocentric axes is more fundamental than his capacity to think in terms of a body im-age. The egocentric identification of places does not depend on a prior identification of a body. The notion of an egocentric frame is more fundamental than the relevant notion of body-centeredness. It is only when we have elucidated the notion of an egocentric frame that we are in a position to say what this notion of body-centeredness is.

How, then, are we to characterize egocentric frames of refer-ence? One alternative approach would be to say that an ego-centric frame is one defined by the axes up, down, left, right, in front, and behind, with the origin identified as here. Places cannot be identified by directions from a single origin alone. We have to add something about the way distances are measured in this frame of reference, or at least we need some kind of order relation. Even so, this approach would not give us enough to say in general what an egocentric frame is. We want to allow as intelligible the hypothesis that humans may use many different egocentric frames. Consider, for example, the axes defining the movements of the hand in writing. There is no reason to suppose that this will be the very same set of axes used to define the movements of the whole body. Nevertheless, it is still an egocentric frame. So an approach that tries to define what it is for a frame to be egocentric by simply listing a particular set of axes will not work. Again, there is no reason to suppose that all species will use the same egocentric axes. For example, creatures that are jointed differently from us or that live deep underwater may use different axes. Finally, even if, by listing a suitable set of axes, we could give an extensionally correct identification of the egocentric frames, we would still have the explanatory work to do. We would still have to explain what it was about the terms 'left' and 'right', for example, that made them particularly connected to moving and acting, for example. Even so, the right way to give a general definition of the notion of an egocentric frame of reference may still be by defining a class of axes, rather than by making a general demand about where the frames must be centered. And, of course, we expect that an extensional approach here will not succeed: we have to grasp how the subject is apprehending those axes.

The axes distinctive of an egocentric frame are those that are immediately used by the subject in the direction of action. They may include, but need not be confined to, the natural axes of the body. In the case of the in-front and behind axis we have a distinction defined in terms of the body and its modes of movement and perception. Its application to us depends on exploiting ways in which we are not symmetrical. If we were symmetrical, being double-jointed and able to look either way, then our current notions of in front and behind simply could not be applied to ourselves, could not guide our actions in the way that they do. But we are not symmetrical in this way, and the distinction does guide our actions. In the case of the up and down axis, we seem not to have here a distinction defined in terms of asymmetries of the body. It has to do rather with orientation in the gravitational field. The extensive apparatus we have to tell us how we are oriented in the gravitational field is precisely the apparatus that tells us which way is up. The reason this matters to us is, of course, the pervasive influence of gravity on every aspect of our ordinary actions. So here we have an egocentric axis not defined as a natural axis of the body. Of course there is the long axis of the body, but this is not the same thing as up and down, which continue to be defined in terms of the gravitational field, even if one is leaning at an angle. The distinction between left and right does not follow either of these models. The fundamental distinction here does not have anything especially to do with the bodily axes at all. It is not, as in the case of in front and behind, that there is any bodily asymmetry that the distinction labels, since animals are generally right-left symmetric. Nor does it label, like 'up' and 'down', some external physical magnitude of general importance for action. Nonetheless, it is evidently an axis used to direct action.

I said that egocentric axes are "immediately" used to direct action. It may be that no very precise definition can be given of this notion of immediate use, and that the notion of an egocentric reference frame must to this extent remain a rough and intuitive one. But we can get some sense of the required conception by contrasting egocentric frames with more complex dead-reckoning systems, that is, systems that enable one to keep track of where one is by keeping track of how fast one has been moving, in what direction, and for how long. The point about such systems that matters here is their use of a compass, which is external to anything used to immediately direct action. For example, an animal might use the position of the sun, together with its knowledge of the time of day, as a compass. It can use the position of the sun to keep track of each of its various swoops and sallies, and so to plot the direct route home. But before it can actually translate this into action, it has to know the direct route home not merely in terms of direction specified in terms of the external compass; it has to know which way to point itself to travel in that direction. It is in this sense that the egocentric axes are immediately used to direct action, whereas the external compass is not. Of course, a dead-reckoning system could also use the egocentric axes themselves, though in practice this would mean a considerable loss in accuracy. Notice, incidentally, that these dead-reckoning systems are body centered; what make them nonegocentric are the axes that they use and the indirectness of their role in guiding action.

So far we have considered one part of the characterization of a frame of reference: the way in which it identifies places at a time. But characterization of a frame of reference must also say what criterion is being used for the identity of places over time. To pinpoint the issues, consider an extremely simple experimental paradigm used by Linda Acredolo (1990) to find out whether and in what way infants identify places. Her experimental space is an enclosure ten feet square with two identical windows across from each other. There is a round table in the center of the room with a buzzer under it and a long moveable rod attached. And the end of the rod is a seat on wheels, which can revolve around the table. On top of the seat is an infant. In the training phase, the buzzer sounds in the center. About five seconds later, an adult appears at one of the windows, calling the child's name and generally entertaining it for five seconds or so. Of course, the child turns to look, and the pairings of buzzer and event, always at the same window, continue until the child has developed an expectation that such an event will follow the buzzer. That is, on hearing the buzzer, the child turns toward the window before the adult appears. After this training phase, the chair is moved around the table to the other side of the room. The buzzer is sounded, and the experimenters watch to see toward which window the child looks in expectation of the event.

Obviously, if the child has learnt merely a spatial response, such as to look to the left, it will look toward the wrong window. There certainly are these spatial behaviors, though they are more primitive than the ability to identify places. For example, there is the ability to reach to the left or the right, or to jump out of the way of an oncoming object. Even if the infant has only a particular response, such as looking to the left, its behavior may still be properly described as spatial. It may vary the type of muscular movement in many different ways, depending on the starting orientation of its body when the buzzer is sounded, so as always to achieve the result of looking to the left. So it may be impossible to describe the response as a nonspatial muscular movement, even though it is more primitive than place identification.

It might indeed be said that in the case in which the child looks at the wrong window, it is using a notion of place on which sameness of place over time is defined by sameness of egocentric coordinates. On this notion of place, no sense can be assigned to the idea that the child itself might be in motion, or capable of movement. Rather, it has an array of places, such as the one "just within reach and to the right," that it carries with it through the world. In this frame, something is said to be in the same place at one moment as at another if at both times it was just within the subject's reach and to the right, whether or not the subject had, as an observer using a more standard frame of reference might say, "moved" in the meantime. We can certainly imagine a subject for whom this is a possibility. For example, an Oriental despot might so arrange matters that however and whenever he moves, there is always Turkish delight just within reach and to the right.

We have finally to consider the case in which the child manages to use the information available to it through the rotation to keep track of the right window and look toward it, even though this means giving a different spatial response, such as looking to the right rather than looking to the left. In this case the child is certainly reidentifying a place, but it is not using sameness of egocentric coordinates over time as the criterion for sameness of place. This raises the question what criterion the child is using. The obvious proposal is that the criterion used is egocentric coordinates plus compensation for the child's own movements. No frame of reference other than the egocentric frame is used.

Acredolo found a gradual transition from looking at the wrong window to looking at the correct window as the children grew older or, more precisely, as the time during which the child was capable of self-locomotion increased. Similar keeping track of a place over time is achieved by the whole class of animals that manage to find their way back home by keeping track of their own movements—the directions and distances of their travel from moment to moment—and then using path integration to find the direct route home (see, for example, Müller and Wehner 1988).

1.3 Maps

As we saw, some people have denied that there is such a thing as objective or absolute space. Empiricism or pragmatism about spatial concepts means that a spatial frame of reference must always be understood in terms of its relation to egocentric space. Poincaré put the point succinctly: "absolute space is nonsense, and it is necessary for us to begin by referring space to a system of axes invariably bound to our body" (1913, 257). This was vigorously rejected by O'Keefe and Nadel:

Most authors attempt to derive all psychological notions of space from an organism's interaction with objects and their relations. The notion of an absolute spatial framework, if it exists at all, is held by these authors to derive from prior concepts of relative space, built up in the course of an organism's interaction with objects or with sensations correlated with objects.

In contrast to this view, we think that the concept of absolute space is primary and that its elaboration does not depend upon prior notions of relative space. . . . [There] are spaces centred on the eye, the head, and the body, all of which can be subsumed under the heading of *egocentric space*. In addition, there exists at least one neural system which provides the basis for an integrated model of the environment. This system underlies the notion of absolute, unitary space, which is a non-centred stationary framework through which the organism and its egocentric spaces move. (1978, 1–2)

Let us consider what the prospects are for finding such an absolute or objective mode of spatial thought. We saw that we cannot define an egocentric space as a body-centered one, but can we not define an allocentric frame of reference to be one centered on something other than the body? Certainly that is in practice often what is meant by 'allocentric', which is a term often opposed to 'egocentric' in the literature.

There are many distinctions to be drawn here. For example, we can ask whether it is possible for a subject to be using only allocentric frames of reference in spatial action. In the case of a patient described by Cole (1991) who has no or only residual proprioception and kinesthesis, for example, the patient describes the extraordinary effort involved in purely visually guided action: taking a visual fix on a point in the room and keeping himself upright and stationary only by maintaining his fix on the point; picking up a glass by remarking its relation to his fixed point, the relation of his hand to the fixed point, and bringing the hand to the glass by varying its relation to the fixed point. It does not seem to be an unintelligible hypothesis that in action the subject may be using only an allocentric frame of reference, one centered on his fixed point, and that there is no immediate use of any body-centered frame of reference. In that case, an allocentric frame of reference would be what is immediately used in guiding action. The allocentric frame would then count as "egocentric" by the definition I reached in section 1.2. This is discordant terminology. The fact is that I am drawing distinctions that the literature obliterates; what matters is that we separate and understand the various classifications that there are. The use of 'egocentric' as defined above is also widespread. The point is that 'body-centred' and 'immediately used in directing action' ordinarily coincide, which is why ordinary vocabulary does not distinguish them.

Would the existence of an allocentric frame of reference, one not centered on the subject and that need not be immediately used to guide action, show that there is an objective level of thought that resists empiricist-pragmatist criticism of the Poincaré type? I can make the question concrete by considering a very simple representative of a whole class of navigational systems (see Cartwright and Collett 1983). This is the triangulation model used by Wilkie and Palfrey (1987) to explain the behavior of rats in a water maze. Rats are placed in a swimming pool filled with an opaque liquid. There is a submerged platform to which they learn to make their way. The platform, being submerged in an opaque liquid, cannot be seen by the rat. But it can reliably make its way to it from any starting point in the pool, so long as it keeps track of its relation to the distinctive landmarks it can see around the pool. The triangulation model supposes that what happens is this: Once on the platform, the animal records the distances to each of the cues it can see. Then when it next tries to get to the platform, it notes the distances from where it is to each of the landmarks around it. If the distance to a landmark is currently greater than it was from the platform goal, the animal swims toward it. If the distance is less than it was from the goal, the animal swims away from it. Its movement is the resultant of all these calculations. The animal using this model certainly has an allocentric representation of spatial relations, in the sense that it uses a frame of reference centered on something other than its own body. It has recorded the distances from the target platform to the cues around it. But it is hard to see why the empiricist or pragmatist should be particularly moved by this. For it is only through its connections to its own perceptions and actions that the animal manages to give any meaning to the spatial information. The allocentric representation has meaning only through its connections with the animal's egocentric space, in the sense of 'egocentric' defined above.

There is another array of distinctions that I should remark on. We already saw that for a creature to be representing places, it must have some grasp of a criterion of identity for places over time. It is a separate question whether it appreciates that the places it represents are all spatially related to one another, whether it grasps the connectedness of the space.

Consider again the child who succeeds in Acredolo's (1990) paradigm. The child is certainly representing places and may be able to represent more than one place at a time, but this does not yet show that it is capable of grasping the spatial relations among the places it can represent.

It would be possible to have a creature or system that simultaneously made explicit all the spatial relations between all the places it could represent. This is a very strong condition. It is also possible to have a creature that, while not meeting this condition, can make explicit a sufficiently rich range of spatial relations and perform sufficiently powerful operations on that base of spatial relations to derive the spatial relations between any two places.

There is a family of conditions here, depending on exactly which spatial relations we have in mind. There can be variations in what the underlying geometry is taken to be. And there are differences in what configurational properties of a network of places the system might be capable of representing.

These issues about the extent to which the connectedness of a space is represented are just different from questions about where the frame of reference is centered. It would be possible to have a system capable of very powerful representation of connectedness centered on the body, for example.

Possession of a map of one's environment is sometimes defined in terms of the strength of the spatial relations that can be represented among the places represented.[1] Mapping abilities in this sense constitute no very evident objection to the empiricist-pragmatist critique of the notion of objective space. I can bring this out by turning to the model of spatial navigation proposed by John O'Keefe.

I will describe O'Keefe's (1990, 1991) model only very schematically. On this model, the *slope-centroid model,* there are two stages in an animal's construction of a map of its environment. The animal identifies a notional point in its environment, the centroid, which is a notional point in the sense in which the South Pole or the Equator are notional: there may be no distinctive physical feature at that place. It is a fixed point, in that it does not move with the animal. The animal also identifies a gradient for its environment, a way of giving compass directions. This is the slope of the environment. It functions like the direction east-west. The direction is fixed no matter how one moves around, and one can partially define which way one is going by saying what angle one is making with it. As in almost all models of mapping, we take it that the animal is constructing a two-dimensional map of its environment; the third dimension is not mapped.

Once the animal has done this, it can construct a map of its environment by recording the vector from the centroid to each of its targets, using the slope to define direction. Suppose that it has done this and now wants to know how to get to a particular target. What it must do is to find the vector from itself to the centroid. Once it has the vector from itself to the centroid and the vector from the centroid to the target, it can find the vector from itself directly to the target.

This certainly gives the animal an allocentric frame of reference, in the sense defined above, for the frame of reference is organized around the centroid, rather than the body of the animal. This is also a geometrically very powerful model, capable of representing many of the spatial relations among the places in its environment. So it will meet any reasonable connectedness condition on maps.

The question that remains is whether the existence and use of such a system constitutes a reply to the empiricist-pragmatist critique of the notion of objective space. Does it fare any better than the triangulation model? We saw that from this point of view, the problem with the triangulation model is that it seems to have meaning for the animal only insofar as it is connected to the animal's perception and action, to its egocentric space. Now the slope-centroid model does seem to be more distanced from perception and action than the triangulation model. The reason is the purely notional character of the slope and centroid, which do not themselves relate directly to perception: they are computed on the basis of it. In contrast, the distinguished point in the triangulation model is the platform goal, which the animal actually occupies and from which it observes the distances to the cues around it. Yet despite the fact that there is this sense in which the slope-centroid model seems to be more remote from perception and action than the triangulation model, it still seems that the model has meaning for the animal only insofar as it is connected to perception and action. The basic point here is quite elementary. The mapping systems we are considering are all navigational systems. Their significance is exhausted by their implications for navigation. It is, therefore, quite impossible that they should constitute objections to the empiricist-pragmatist critique of objective space. If we want to find examples of genuinely objective spatial thought, we have to look for modes of spatial thought whose role lies not only in the demands of navigation.

1.4 Physical Objects and Objective Space

The fundamental point in all this is that we cannot ascribe spatial representations to animals in a way that outruns their capacity to give causal significance to the representations. And the distinctions that matter are distinctions in the way causal significance is assigned. I want to elaborate on this point before returning to the characterization of objective space.

We can distinguish between a pure geometry, which is a purely formal exercise in mathematical computation, and an applied geometry, which is a body of doctrine about the world in which we live. What turns one into the other is the assignation of some physical meaning to the spatial concepts, for example, the identification of a straight line as the path of a light ray *in vacuo*. So, to find what about spatial reasoning makes it reasoning about the space one is in, we must look for an account of the laws or regularities, however probabilistic or open to exception, that connect spatial properties with other physical properties. To do this is not to demand definitions of spatial concepts in terms of other physical concepts. We cannot assume that spatial concepts are less primitive than any others, and we cannot assume that we can separate out, from the flux of physical thinking, some regularities that alone deserve to be elevated into definitions. There may be no definitions to be had (M. Friedman 1983). Still, insofar as spatial reasoning is to be understood as reasoning about one's actual environment, rather than as pure geometry, it is theoretical. It is only its figuring in an intuitive physics of one's environment, through regularities connecting spatial properties with other physical properties, that makes it reasoning that is not purely mathematical but rather about the space in which one lives.

We also have to explain why an animal's capacity to engage in spatial reasoning might have been selected for under evolutionary pressure. And if the reasoning has no physical significance, it cannot help the animal to cope with its surroundings and thus has no selection value. We ought to be reluctant to ascribe spatial reasoning when its use by the organism defies explanation in terms of selection pressures. If we subscribe to an evolutionary-teleological view of content—ascription (as in Millikan 1984), we will not simply be reluctant to do this but regard it as incoherent to do so. Of course, there are views on which spatial reasoning is simply a form of causal reasoning: spatial notions can in some sense be reduced to, or explained in terms of, causal notions (Sklar 1983, van Fraassen 1985). But we can accept the need for us to relate a creature's ability to represent space, to its capacity to give physical significance to those spatial representations, without insisting on any such reductionist thesis. We can even accept that spatial notions have to be used in elucidating the concept of cause (Salmon 1984). It seems unlikely that there will be any firm formal rule governing the connection between the spatial content of reasoning and the physical interpretation assigned to such content, just as in physics there is no firm formal rule governing the physical meaning that a theory must assign to a spatial magnitude. All we can do is to look at the ways in which particular theories use particular spatial magnitudes and, case by case, argue that this or that one has or has not been assigned sufficient physical meaning.

Suppose, now, we ask what use one makes of grasp of the fact that every place in one's environment is spatially related to every other place in it. The answer is that we have to look at the physical significance one assigns to this relatedness, at the way one grasps the causal connectedness of space. Because of what I will call their *internal causal connectedness,* physical objects play a special role in how we register the connectedness of space. The internal causal connectedness of objects means that the possibility of their traveling through a space can give physical significance to its spatial connectedness.

What does it mean to say that physical objects are internally causally connected? The point is that the condition of a thing at any one time is causally dependent upon its condition at earlier times. Grasp of this idea is presupposed in an understanding of the way in which objects interact with one another. If we are to have any appreciation at all of the effect that one object can have on another in a collision, for example, we have to understand that one determinant of the way the thing will be after the collision is the way that very thing was before the collision. The result of the impact may be a smash or a bounce; which result happens will depend in part on how brittle the object was to begin with. The way the object is later depends in part on the way it was earlier, and we have to grasp this if we are further to grasp that the earlier condition of an object is only a partial determinant of the way it is now and that external factors may have played a role. So in describing our ordinary thought about physical objects, we need a distinction between the causality that is internal to the object and has to do with the dependence of its later stages on its earlier ones and the causality that has to do with the external relations between objects and the ways in which they act upon each other.

Even if we consider a physical object through a period in which it is not involved in any interactions, it remains true that its condition through any interval in that period causally depends on its condition in earlier intervals. This is so whether the condition of the object remains stable during the period or is inherently subject to some variation, such as a decay process.

In this matter, objects can be contrasted with, for example, shadows. Even if a shadow remains constant through a period or undergoes only regular variation, its condition at times through that interval does not causally depend on its condition at earlier times. Rather, the condition of the shadow at any time depends directly on the way things are with the light source, occluders and surfaces. It does not depend on how things were with the shadow earlier. So unlike physical objects, shadows are not internally causally connected. The same point could be made about, for example, the spot of light cast by a searchlight on a wall, which is like a shadow in not being internally causally connected.

Philosophers interested in causation have tried to use this point about physical objects in analyzing causation; philosophers interested in the identities of physical things have tried to use this point in analyzing object identity.[2] But without attempting to analyze either causation or object identity, I can say what is the bearing of this point on the way in which we give causal significance to the spatial connectedness of a region. The internal causal connectedness of physical things means that they can give physical meaning to spatial connectedness. In particular, the possibility of an object's moving from one place to another means that we can see how the way things are at one place could causally depend on the way they were at another place. For example, if a horse plods from the start of a track to its end, the way things are at the end of the track now causally depends upon the way they were at the start. When we consider the movements of objects through a space as causally connecting one place with another, if we further consider the details of that movement, we can see how to give physical significance to the metric for the space within our intuitive physics. The crucial notion here is the time taken for the object to reach a particular destination from a particular starting point, given what sort of thing it is and what causes are affecting its movement. These remarks only begin to sketch the structure given to the space of our intuitive physics by physical things. The continuity of object movement means that an order is imposed on the places between starting point and destination, depending on the trajectory we ascribe to the object, and this order in turn is responsible to our conception of the causes of the movement of the object. None of this can be achieved by considering shadows alone. Just because they are not internally causally connected, shadows cannot be used to give causal significance to the spatial connectedness of a region. The movement of a shadow from one place to another is not a way of ensuring that the way things are at the destination is causally dependent on the way things were at the starting point.

So much for the role of thought about physical things in giving causal significance to the spatial connectedness of a region. I want now to remark that there seems to be a level of thought more primitive than our thought about physical objects, and to consider how connectedness might be thought about at that level. This primitive level of thought is perhaps exemplified by the way in which we ordinarily think about the stars. If we are asked, as we look at the night sky and try to identify constellations, whether we think of the stars as physical objects or as points of light with no more causal significance than shadows, we may have no immediate answer. We are not really thinking of them as either; the question had not come up before. We were at a more primitive level of thought than this. So it may be an effort to recall astronomical knowledge from school. That is, I think, part of the reason why men landing on the moon was such a shock. It is not just the distances involved. It forced us very directly to think of the moon as a physical thing, and this is not ordinarily forced so vividly upon us.

Consider now the case of an animal swimming in the water maze, using the triangulation model and the cues hung around the pool to navigate to the platform goal. How must the animal be thinking of the cues hung around the pool? Must it be thinking of them as physical objects, or might it be thinking of them as more like shadows or points of light? There is no reason why the animal should have had to make up its mind about this. They are recognizable and stably at those places, and this is really all the animal needs.

Nevertheless, as we saw, the animal using the triangulation model does manage to give causal significance to the spatial relations between various places in the space it is in, even if it does not manage to register the full connectedness of the space. But evidently, it cannot be doing this in the way I have just been describing, exploiting the internal causal connectedness of physical objects, since it may not be capable of thinking in terms of physical objects at all but rather be operating at a more primitive level of thought. So how is it managing to give causal significance to spatial notions? It does not do this by reflective causal thinking at all. It does this through its own engagement in the space: not by thinking about its engagement in the space but by putting the triangulation model to work in navigating itself through the space. I could talk about a *practical* interpretation of the spatial notions used in the triangulation. This makes very obvious why thought at the level of the triangulation model cannot be described as objective or absolute spatial thinking. For such thought gets its physical significance only through its relation to the subject's perception and action, only through its relation to his egocentric space.

Let us now consider the model of slope and centroid. What motivates the idea that this is a peculiarly objective or absolute type of thought? What makes this seem plausible is that the vectors from the centroid to the cues in the environment do not depend on the current location of the animal. The animal can record these vectors and carry that map around with it. This is why we seem to have a level of thinking here that does not have to be explained in terms of its relations to the animal's perception and action, to its egocentric space.

It is striking, however, that if we ask whether the animal using the model of slope and centroid must be thinking of the cues as physical objects, the answer is no. It may be using the primitive level of thought that we can use when thinking about the stars, at which the distinction between objects and shadows is not yet drawn. It need not be thinking of the cues as internally causally connected. It may, for example, have no expectations whatever as to what would happen if two of the cues collided. The way in which causal significance is being assigned to the spatial notions is not through the thought of the things around it as physical objects.

There is a contrast between the cues that an animal uses as landmarks in navigating around and its targets in navigation. There is no need for the animal itself to interact with any of the landmarks except by perceiving them. But the target, its destination through the navigation, typically will be something with which the animal interacts. It may be food or a nest or a mate or prey or its young. Here it does not seem right to say that the animal might as well be thinking of these things as shadows. It expects its young, once fed, to stay fed for a while, and when it eats, it expects this to have some persisting effect on it. It need not have a reflective understanding of these points, but it does have to have some practical grasp of them. The reason that it does not need a reflective grasp of these points is that it is using its own interactions with the targets to constitute its grasp of their causal significance.

Certainly the animal is not using reflective thought about its targets to assign causal significance to spatial relations: it does this rather through the fact of its own engagement in the space. The slope-centroid model is in this regard in exactly the same position as the triangulation model. It is true that the vectors from the centroid to various cues do not depend upon the location of the animal. But when we subtract the animal, we also subtract any physical meaning for those vectors. The vectors get their meaning only when the animal is plugged in. They have causal significance only through their relations to the animal's perception and action, to its egocentric space.

At this point it is not hard to see what is required of an objective or absolute representation of space. What is right about the empiricist-pragmatist critique is that spatial notions must be given causal significance. The mistake is to think that this can be done only through one's own interactions in space. What we need is a way of registering the connectedness of a space in a way that does not depend upon the subject's own engagement in the space. And we have seen why physical objects might be expected to play a crucial role here. There are, of course, many other phenomena than the movements of physical things that in diverse ways transmit the effects of things being thus and so at one place to their being thus and so at another place. For example, there are the everyday phenomena of magnetism, heat and cold, the flow of liquids, and the winds. One fundamental range of alternatives to physical objects emerges if we consider a mariner navigating in a vast circuit of tides, whirlpools, eddies, and currents. It is open to him, in principle at any rate, to register the physical significance of the spatial connectedness of the region he is in without exploiting his own navigation through the space or introducing the notion of a physical object. The waves themselves, propagated through the space and interacting with one another in endlessly complex ways, demand for their understanding a rich grasp of the connectedness of the space. In our commonsense understanding of the world, we can, to some extent, use this kind of causal thinking on land, as when we watch the effects of an earthquake or the impact of a sledge hammer on the wall of a house. But these phenomena are not sufficiently pervasive in our experience to provide the full strength of our grasp of the theoretical significance of the connectedness of the space we occupy. What we have to investigate now, and what I will begin on in the next chapter, is the way in which one's conception of one's life as extending over time, a time in which one has a current temporal orientation, depends on this ability to form an objective conception of the space one is in. This is what explains the value of objective spatial thinking for us.

1.5   Common Causes and Informative Identities

In *Individuals* (1959), Strawson held that reidentification of places depends on the reidentification of things. We identify places by their relations to things; we see that we are once again between Black Mountain and the lake, for example. In view of the dependence of the reidentification of places on the reidentification of things, Strawson said, "The fact that material bodies are the basic particulars in our scheme can be deduced from the fact that our scheme is of a certain kind, viz. the scheme of a unified spatiotemporal system of one temporal and three spatial dimensions."[3] This thesis is certainly too strong as it stands. An animal might use a set of cues to identify and reidentify places without ever raising the question of whether they are processes or pseudoprocesses; the animal might operate at a level of thought that is more primitive than that at which a distinction is marked between a shadow and a thing, since a stable shadow will do as well as a thing when reidentifying places.

Nevertheless, it can hardly be denied that our reference to places is densely interwoven with reference to things and that reference to things greatly enhances our capacity for reference to places. This is principally because of the possibility of perception-based informative identities of physical things. On recognizing the identity of Mount Afla with Mount Ateb, for example, one opens up the possibility of relating all the places one had identified using Afla to all the places one had identified using Ateb. One can now grasp the spatial relations of all these places to one another. Again, it can happen that, lost in a town one has just come to, one suddenly realizes that one is staring at an unfamiliar angle of a building one knows perfectly well and so can find one's way from there.

To understand such happenings, we have to bear in mind a further causal dimension to physical objects other than that they are internally causally connected. This is the capacity of a physical thing to function as a common cause of many different effects. To make the point vivid, I will move away from cases of ordinary navigation and look instead at an astronomical example. Consider the case of the twin quasars $0975 + 561$ A and B. These objects are close together in space, much closer than seems likely, given the scatter of the other known quasars, and their spectra are indistinguishable. The similarity here is rather unlikely, and it has an obvious explanation. Namely, we should assume that the minor discrepancies in the information we have about the two quasars are due simply to the margin of error in our methods and that the quasars actually have all their properties in common; that there is just one quasar there. This kind of reasoning is absolutely standard in cases in which an informative identity is discovered. We find that two things are highly similar; we explain the similarity by postulating an identity of objects and remarking that by Leibniz's law, they therefore have all their properties in common.

I must also remark, though, that there is another way of reading the case of the twin quasars. We have two images of the quasars with an astonishing correlation in the information they contain about the quasar that is their source. This correlation we explain by the fact that there is a common cause of both images. Since the same thing causes the production of both, the correlation is intelligible. In the case of the quasars, what happens is that a galaxy intervening between the quasar and us splits the light, and consequently the image. These are two quite different descriptions of the same example. The problem is not to choose between them, for surely both are illuminating. The problem is to understand how they can both be correct and to understand the relation between them.

What are the effects that the quasar is being said to be a common cause of? The obvious answer is the production of two images of itself at some spatial separation. The similarity between the two images, then, is what requires explanation in terms of a single common cause. Observe, though, that it is not crucial to the example that there should be an intrinsic similarity between the images themselves; the similarity that matters in the reasoning that leads one to the conclusion of identity is a similarity between the quasars represented. To suppose that this similarity can be represented only if we have some intrinsic similarity between the images themselves is just a mistake. Representation of similarity need not imply similarity of representation (Millikan 1991). The principle of the common cause is being invoked to explain why there is the otherwise improbable correlation between the content of the image of the one quasar and the content of the image of its twin.

The case of the quasar is somewhat unusual among cases of informative identities in that there is explicit reflection on the character of the images formed and the resemblances between them. In the case of the Morning Star and the Evening Star, there may be no such reflection on our perceptual images. We may simply remark, on the basis of our perception of the sky, that the Morning Star and the Evening Star have much in common and then appeal to identity and Leibniz's law to explain the commonality. But even so, the principle of the common cause is still in play. For the properties that we note the two bodies to have in common must be causally significant. And the identity statement, that the Morning Star is the Evening Star, is not true unless the cause of one's perception of the one heavenly body is the same as the cause of one's perception of the other heavenly body. There is, then, a sense in which the reasoning behind an ordinary informative identity in which there is no reflection on the perceptions of the object nevertheless depends upon the principle of the common cause. The ground-floor reasoning is correct only if the reflective recapitulation, which refers to the perceptions and explicitly uses the principle of the common cause, also correct.

2

The Past

2.1 Temporal Orientation

Suppose you are lost and finally pull out a map and try to get your bearings, an ordinary ordnance-survey map, say. What you have to do is to bring the information on the map into some kind of congruence with the the spatial information that you have from perception. The map uses one frame of reference, the ordnance-survey reference grid, to specify spatial relations. Through vision, you know that some things are near, some farther away, some up and to the left, some in front, and some behind. What you have to do is bring the two systems into congruence, so that you can say, 'This is the telephone box here, the church is a good way behind us, and that is Wheatley over there. So the path must be off to the left down here.' When you manage that, you have oriented yourself with the frame of reference used in the map.

Can we make sense of a similar procedure in the case of time? Can we make sense of the idea of there being temporal frames of reference with which we orient ourselves? We can. Take, for example, the question so often hotly disputed by clergymen: 'Which day of the week is it?' (Some affect indifference, but it is rarely genuine.) Here the problem is to orient oneself with respect to another frame of reference, so that one can say, 'Yesterday was Tuesday, so tomorrow is Thursday, and in four days it will be the Sabbath.' One uses such terms as 'today' and 'tomorrow' in orienting oneself in the temporal frame of reference just as in the case of spatial orientation one uses 'here' and 'over there' in orienting oneself using the map. There are also parallels in the strategies one uses to keep oneself oriented. For example, one may keep track of landmark days, such as the Sabbath, or use methods that enable one to tell directly whether this is Wednesday (W. Friedman 1990).

We have to mark a fundamental distinction between the two types of temporal orientation, both of which use tensed temporal indicators. One is what I will call *temporal orientation with respect to phase*. The other is what I will call *temporal orientation with respect to particular time*. Temporal orientation with respect to phase is much more primitive. Consider an animal that hibernates. Through the part of the year for which it is awake, it regulates its activity depending on the season. Such an animal certainly has a use for temporal orientation. It can recognize that it is now late spring, perhaps by keeping track of how long it has been since winter, and realize that it will soon be summer. But it may not have the conception of the seasons as particular times; it may be incapable of differentiating between the autumn of one year and the autumn of another. It simply has no use for the conception of a particular autumn, as opposed to the general idea of the season. So while this animal is capable of orientation with respect to phases, it is not capable of orientation with respect to particular times.

In contrast, our ordinary keeping track of days of the week really is orientation with respect to particular times. We think in terms not just of yesterday having been Tuesday but also of its having been Tuesday three weeks ago. We think in terms of particular Tuesdays, and we have the general conception of that day of the week. We can, for example, think of what happened on one Tuesday as causally affecting what happened on a later Tuesday, whereas it may be quite impossible for our hibernating animal to think of what happened one autumn as causally affecting what happened on a later autumn.

As we saw when I discussed spatial frames of reference, the basic distinctions have to do with the way in which the framework is given causal significance. Here too we can look at the ways in which the notions of time are given causal significance by the creature using them. Again, we are not looking for definitions or reductions of temporal notions; all that we want is to see how temporal notions figure in the creature's primitive physics of its environment. If an animal is to be said to be using the notion of two things being simultaneous, for example, it is certainly legitimate to ask what causal meaning it assigns to the relation, what use its physics makes of the relation.

It is not just that there is a parallel here between spatial and temporal frames of reference: there is a *connection*. The type of causal thinking needed for one to be using a temporal framework that operates in terms in terms of particular times rather than phases is the kind of causal thinking needed for one to be thinking in terms of what in the last chapter I called an objective or absolute frame of spatial reference. The fundamental distinction I drew in the last chapter was the distinction between giving causal significance to a spatial frame through one's own engagement in the space and having a reflective or detached understanding of the causal meaning of spatial notions. When we consider grasp of temporal notions, it seems immediately apparent that grasp of the causal significance of past temporal relations cannot be exhausted by a practical understanding of its implications for future action. To give causal significance to the temporal relations between past events, one needs a reflective understanding of causation. We will see in later chapters that this reflective understanding of causation is what one needs if one is to be not just an agent interacting with one's environment but is also to be capable of achieving a detached understanding of the causal relations between oneself and one's surroundings, if one is to be self-conscious.

One question we will have to consider is the role of episodic memory in providing such an understanding of the past tense, as relating not to phases but to particular past times. I will be interpreting 'episodic memory' to mean memory of a past happening conceived as having a particular past time at which it took place. This might be understood liberally so as to include, say, the memory of a walk I used to take one summer. The memory of the walk may be bound up with the memory of that summer, but it may be that what I recall is not any particular time I took that walk but the walk itself. I will still count this as episodic, because it exploits one's grasp of the concept of the past. In contrast, consider the delayed condition-discrimination experiments, which have sometimes been held to display possession of episodic memory (Olton 1984). In these experiments an animal learns that it will be shown a stimulus, the stimulus will be withdrawn, and then which reaction obtains a reward will depend on what the stimulus was. If the animal manages to react appropriately, it is said, this must be because it remembers what the stimulus was. But this will not be an episodic memory in my sense, because such an experiment evidently does nothing to show that the animal has a temporal frame of reference. The animal certainly manages to store the character of the token stimulus that was presented, but that does not show that it manages to conceive of the stimulus presentation as having happened at some particular past time. In contrast, when I remember that talk we had on a summer evening so long ago, I may well be hazy about which summer it was, but that it happened some summer is not in question, so my memory will still count as episodic.

Our topic is the way in which causal significance is given to the temporal framework presupposed by episodic memory. I have already suggested that we will need a distinction between a reflective understanding of causation and a practical grasp of it. But a grasp of the possibilities here demands that I have a richer grasp of just what might be available in a practical physics. So in the next section, I will look at that. Then I will consider the kinds of physical significance that might be given to temporal notions.

2.2 Primitive Physics: Causal Indexicality and Working Concepts

In this section I want to reflect on the character of our most primitive physical thinking: our sense of the physics of our environment that we exercise in everyday interactions with it, such as lighting a fire, throwing a rock, or putting up an umbrella. One type of question concerns the structure of this physics: whether there is an underlying core theory whose tenets are heavily qualified by experience or whether it is rather a patchwork of a million different pieces. But the issues about time that concern us are, I think, independent even of that question. What concerns us is something still more fundamental. We have to look at the kinds of concepts that have to be used in formulating a primitive physics and then ask how temporal notions could be given significance in such a context.

At this point we have to leave behind Gilbert Ryle's dichotomy between knowing how and knowing that. Someone in the grip of this dichotomy faces a dilemma. On the one hand, he can say that grasp of a primitive physics is simply a matter of knowing how to get on, knowing how to get around in and manipulate one's environment. But then he seems to be cut off from giving any cognitive description of what is going on. This is the point of saying that this is knowing how rather than knowing that. But the phenomena here are cognitive. On the other hand, he may say that grasp of an intuitive physics is not just a matter of knowing how, it really is a matter of knowing that. But then he may feel bound to give over-intellectualized descriptions of what are after all very primitive capacities that we have. We can avoid this latter danger by paying attention to the concepts we use in formulating the content of knowing that.

Let us look, then, at the kinds of concepts involved. First, I want to point out the possibility of a kind of indexicality. Indexical terms are those that vary their reference, depending systematically upon the context in which they are used. It may be that all uses of words are context-dependent, but then what is special about indexicals that their reference is systematically so dependent. For example, 'now' refers to the time at which it is used. So when it is used at different times, it refers to different times. It is, as we might say, temporally indexical. What it refers to depends on the time of utterance. 'Yesterday' is another temporal indexical. In contrast, 'here', in one way of using it, refers to wherever the speaker is when he uses it. So it refers to different places when used in different contexts. We could say that it is spatially indexical, in that its reference depends on spatial features of the context of utterance. And any token of 'I' refers to whoever produced it, so different tokens of it refer to different people. We could say that it is "personally" indexical.

There are some terms that can be said to be causally indexical. Their reference depends upon the causal powers of the speaker, on just what the speaker is capable of doing. I will give some examples first, before giving a more general description of the class. The easiest way to construct causally indexical terms is by the use of the first person. For example, consider the predicate 'is a weight I can easily lift'. Judgements made using this notion, about whether an object is a weight I can easily lift, have immediate implications for my own actions, for whether I will bother to attempt to attempt to lift the thing in question. Or again, a judgement such as 'This is too hot for me to handle' has immediate implications for my own actions with respect to the thing; the predicate 'is too hot for me to handle' is again causally indexical. These examples might suggest that the distinction here is between predicates whose causal significance varies from subject to subject. For example, whether the predicate 'is too hot for me to handle' applies to a thing depends upon who the subject is. But the application of the predicate 'is magnetic' is not relative to a subject in this way. This, though, does not give us quite the contrast we want. The predicate 'has the same mass as I do' varies in its application, depending upon who is using it. But it has no immediate implications for action. The significance for one's own actions of something's having the same mass as one does oneself depends entirely on further beliefs that one has, such as whether things having the same mass as oneself will be easy or difficult to lift. We want to separate off those predicates whose reference has to do with the immediate implications for one's own actions and reactions to the world.

Let us consider the examples a little further. The predicates 'is a weight I can easily lift' and 'is too hot for me to handle' both use the first person. But intuitively, the use of causally indexical predicates does not depend on self-consciousness. Even a creature that did not grasp the first person could use causally indexical representations. So there ought to be other examples of causally indexical predicates. Further, the predicates 'is a weight I can easily lift' and 'is too hot for me to handle' use notions of weight and temperature that we ought to pause over. Used notions need not themselves be causally indexical; they may rather be on a par with a notion such as magnetic. Whether two things are the same weight or temperature, and what their particular weights or temperatures are, may be definable entirely in nonindexical terms. The complex predicates I have constructed may be using nonindexical physical notions to define causally indexical terms. But on the face of it, one might grasp causally indexical terms without having any grasp of these nonindexical notions. If this is correct, there ought to be more primitive examples of causally indexical terms. These would not be defined in terms of nonindexical physical notions, and they would not use the first person. It seems immediately obvious that there are such more primitive terms for weight and heat. Unstructured uses of 'is heavy' and 'is hot' may relate to the causal impact of the thing upon the subject, rather than being uses of some observer-independent system of classification. Or again, a notion such as being within reach seems to have immediate implications for the subject's actions. The most immediate effect of judgements made using this notion is that the subject will try to contact things within reach but will not try to contact things judged to be out of reach. This predicate is not a first-person one. A creature could use representations of things as within reach or out of reach without having the ability to think using the first person.

In ordinary English, there is a certain social pull in our use of these terms. If we say simply that something is heavy, this may be heard as having to do not with its relation to one's own powers but rather with its relation to the powers of a normal human or with some reference class of objects of the same general type. I want to set aside this phenomenon. We often do need to consider causal indexicals that have to do simply with the relation of the thing to the subject's own powers. In English, the way in which we make this explicit is by use of the first person. But we may want to use a term so restricted when reporting the reasoning of an animal that is not self-conscious. For example, an animal may reliably perform a task even though we vary a number of parameters, but then it may give up at some point. The ball has been thrown too far for the dog to recover, the stick is too heavy for it to lift. In such cases we can test for just why the animal is not attempting the task, and we have to be able to say, for example, that it is because the ball seems to have been thrown too far or the stick seems too heavy. And these notions of too far and too heavy are related only to the subject's own powers, even though the animal may not be self-conscious.

In these cases, it is not just that grasp of the term requires the ability to register when it applies. It is rather that one uses one's grasp of the causal significance of the term in reacting to recognition that it applies. So, for instance, one uses a grasp of the notion of being within reach not simply by differentially responding to cases where something is within reach, which might be done by simply looking confident, for example, just when something is within reach but by the way one moves and acts. Similarly, one uses a grasp of the notions heavy and hot not simply by responding differentially to heaviness and heat but by differences in the ways in which one prepares to lift something heavy or to touch something hot. I might put the point by saying that one's behavior makes it evident that one knows heavy things take more effort to lift, or that putting two heavy things together will make the resultant package impossible to lift, rather than less heavy. But this gives an excessively reflective account of one's grasp of the causal significance of heaviness. For there may be a certain lack of generality in a creature's grasp of causal significance here. A creature may grasp the significance of weight for its own actions but be unable to apply the notion in connection with the actions of other creatures. This tying of causal significance to the creature using the notion is characteristic of causally indexical terms.

I now want to consider a phenomenon that is both related to and in contrast with causal indexicality: the use of what I will call *working concepts*. Here we are considering terms whose reference need not depend on the causal powers of the speaker, but a grasp of whose causal significance does involve the causal powers of the speaker. This distinction between the reference of a term and grasp of its causal significance is familiar from, for example, such notions as that of an electron. Here we have a term that referred to the very same thing through many changes in the conceptions that scientists had of its causal significance as they developed new models of its functioning (Putnam 1975b). A practical analogue of this may be true of our grasp of certain spatial concepts. For example, an understanding of 'here' does not require that its reference should be seen to depend on the causal powers of the speaker, but as we saw, a grasp of the causal significance of a use of 'here' can draw on the causal powers of the creature that uses it. More exactly, though, the phenomenon I want to describe is not peculiarly linguistic. We can talk about working concepts being used even by animals that have no language.

Many concepts are causally significant. One way to think of this is as a matter of their bearing on our ability to make explicitly causal judgements of the form 'x caused y'. We think of ourselves as building up a detailed, reflective picture of the causal relations holding in our world and of our own place in that causal nexus. But there are cases in which one's grasp of the causal significance of a notion doesn't have to do with any detached picture but rather consists in one's practical grasp of its implications for one's own actions. These are working concepts. In the *Physics*, Aristotle gives some early examples. We can contrast a theoretical understanding of the causal properties of particular types of wood, for example, or different metals, such as iron or silver, with the understanding possessed by the carpenter or metalworker. The artisan's grasp of causal properties is not a matter of having a detached picture of them. It has to do rather with the structure of his practical skills: the particular way in which he deals with various types of wood or how he uses different metals. The detached theorist need not have these skills. It is in characterizing the propositional knowledge of the carpenter or metalworker that we have to use working concepts. The subject's grasp of such a notion has to do with his practical grasp of its implications for his own actions.

The artisan need not have any very rich vocabulary for the properties of the wood or metal about which he has knowledge. In training an apprentice, he may say simply, 'When the wood is like this, you have to be careful of that', accompanied by suitable gestures and actions. But he can recognize those properties when he comes across them. His grasp of their causal significance need not be reflectively expressed; it may consist entirely in his practical ability to respond suitably to their presence. But this practical ability should not be thought of as something static; it may be something developed and varied through years of experience in working with woods, just as, at the reflective level, the scientist may over the years change his theoretical model of the electron. It may be that over the years the carpenter keeps constant which particular property of the wood he identifies when he says, 'It's like this', but changes his practice in responding to it. So we have the reference held constant with, as it were, variation in the "theory," or, better, in his practical grasp of the causal significance of the property. This means that his way of thinking of the property is not causally indexical, in the way indicated earlier, because the reference of the term does not depend on his causal powers. Other carpenters might identify the very same property as he does but respond to it in practice in very different ways, disagreeing with his approach, perhaps being explicit in their disagreement. But although this way of thinking of the property is not causally indexical, it is still true that grasp of its causal significance is essential to grasp of what the property is and that the grasp of causal significance is not an explicit, reflective grasp but consists in possession of suitable practical skills.

Someone using a primitive physics need not have a richly elaborated vocabulary for describing actions. Often in practice we fall back on demonstratives. 'If you want the egg whites to stiffen, you have to do this', one might say, suiting the action to the word. The other person, seeing what I am doing, may try to do it too, though we may disagree over whether he is successful. The demonstrative 'this', referring to a type of action, may be used univocally to refer to that type of action both as performed by oneself, and so known otherwise than by observation, and as performed by others (Meltzoff 1990b).

In fact, a creature using a primitive physics need not have even these minimal resources for reference to actions. A squirrel interacting with a nut does not have to have demonstratives to refer to its own actions. But it does need to be able to think about the nut, to identify its causally indexical properties, and to use working concepts. It must be able to identify the nut as edible though surrounded by a crackable shell, for example. It does not need to be able to think about what it is going to do about all this; it simply does it. A practical grasp of the properties of the nut means that it can bring about the desired result. But this does not require that the animal should have any conception of the way in which it brings about the desired result, nor that it should have any conception of the action involved, even simply as 'this'. So a practical grasp does not require that the animal should be able to think of the action as causing its upshot. All the animal has to be able to think about is the upshot. This means that we lack generality here, for the thought of other creatures operating in the same way is not yet provided. All we have is the animal's knowledge of how to bring about the result itself, which is more primitive than a capacity to think about its own actions.

This point needs some elaboration. How are we to think of the way in which we control the movements that constitute our actions? There are many muscle groups in the body. Should we suppose that central commands are sent out from some central organizer to each and every muscle involved in an action? This would put an immense burden on the central system, so large that it becomes improbable. An alternative possibility is that individual muscle groups are organized together into harmoniously performing subsystems. They are harmonious in that they do not compete with one another to try to perform "impossible actions"; there are many restrictions on what they will

attempt. Given that we think of these peripheral units as themselves being highly organized, what kinds of central commands
ought we to think of as being sent from the central system to
control their performance? One possibility is that the central
system simply specifies the destinations of the movements
(Scott Kelso 1982). It does not need to know where the arm is
before the movement begins; it needs only to specify where the
arm has to get to, and the muscle group itself is so organized
as to be able to do the rest. An example sometimes given to
illustrate this possibility is a spring balance. Putting a particular
weight on the end of the balance in effect specifies an extension
for the spring at which it will reach equilibrium. It does not
matter just how far the spring was extended before that end
point was specified; the weight at the end of the balance determines the end point anyway. Of course, we can contrast various ways in which destinations might be described. For
example, we can contrast absolute with relative descriptions.
One might want to lift the weight on the ground to a position
on the bench. This specifies an absolute starting point and end
point. Alternatively, one might simply want to lift the weight
an arm's length higher than it is, no matter where exactly it is
to start with. This is a relative description of the destination of
the action.

Now think of how, at the level of our own ordinary psychology, we think of the destinations of our actions. We do not
think purely in spatial terms here; we use a whole network of
concepts to specify the destinations of our actions. We want
to clear this desk of papers, to lift this heavy weight, to put
some topspin on this tennis ball. There is a whole network
of interconnected concepts that we use to specify the destinations of our actions. This network of concepts is, as it were,
theoretically interconnected. There is no one movement or set

of movements appropriate to lifting a heavy weight; everything depends on whether it is also large or small, with the weight evenly or unevenly distributed throughout its mass. What is distinctive about this network of concepts is that the whole theory has its meaning through its role in the direction of action. The concepts have the contents they do through their connections to action, even though it is not possible to reduce any one concept to any particular set of motor routines.

This point blocks any attempt to deny that causally indexical and working concepts are genuinely part of content, to hold that all we have here is a set of complex behavioral skills. This reductionism would hold that we should just describe the behavior and let the content go. This would be the correct procedure if there were just one, or a small set, of concisely describable motor routines through which the creature using these concepts could go. But this is not the case for the reasonably skilled performer. Exactly what a creature does, given the description of its surroundings in practical terms, depends on exactly what its goals are. And there is no bound on the goals that a creature may have. This purpose relativity of practical skills, together with the theoretical interconnectedness of causally indexical and working concepts, means that we cannot give a simple behavioral reduction of them.

2.3 Timing Systems

What we have to consider now is the way in which a primitive physics gives causal meaning to concepts of time. Ultimately, we have to look at the way in which physical significance is given to representations of particular past times. The question is whether we can make sense of the idea of giving physical significance to representations of particular past times through our development of practical skills. It would seem that the only way in which one can give causal meaning to thoughts about what happened at particular past times is through reflective thought about the network of things that happened and their causal relations to one another. Any purely practical interpretation of the temporal notions cannot give proper place to the idea that these are concepts of what happened at particular past times, rather than being simply a pool of data exhausted by their implications for future action.

To put this point in context, let us look at the practical use of another kind of time representation: representation of elapsed intervals. Suppose that a bird feeds from plants that regenerate their nectar after each raid upon them, and suppose that the bird feeds from plants dispersed over a wide area. Then the bird has a problem. If it returns to a particular plant too soon after its last visit, not enough nectar will have been regenerated to make the trip worthwhile. On the other hand, if it delays its return to the plant, it runs the risk that some other harvester will get to the regenerated nectar first. What the animal needs to solve this problem is the ability to measure elapsed intervals, an internal stopwatch. It has to be able to record elapsed intervals, to compute the time that will give it the maximum rate of return on its visits to these regenerating plants. This is the solution to that problem found by the long-tailed hermit hummingbird in the Costa Rican jungle (Gallistel 1990, 288–291). Its grasp of temporal intervals is not causally indexical. That is, the duration of the interval being measured does not depend on powers of the creature measuring the interval; the interval is not defined by what actions the creature can perform during it. Rather, the concept of a particular interval being used here seems to be a working concept, of the type modeled by Aristotle's artisans. The animal uses a fixed measure of the interval and may very its estimate of what it can do during that time as a result of trial and error.

Again I have to acknowledge that practical significance can readily be given to concepts of temporal order, of one thing happening and then another. Indeed, these practical concepts of temporal order will be needed if the animal is to engage in actions of any complexity at all. Some use of practical concepts of time order is needed by anyone making tea, for example: you have to realize that you boil the water before you pour it from the kettle into the teapot. But this does not put to work the conception of particular past times.

It is instructive to consider how close one can get to representation of particular past times through the use of one's circadian clock. The cycle of night and day is so long-established that these biological clocks are pervasive among earth species. So, consider an animal that has such a clock. It can record the phase of day at which something happens and use that in framing its expectations as to what will happen when. So if it finds food at a particular place at a particular time on one day will expect food to be at that place at that time on succeeding days. Does this mean that the animal can put to work a conception of particular past times? Before trying to answer that, let me give a fuller description of what we are ascribing to the animal to begin with. The internal circadian clock may be an oscillator, something that simply repeats the same process over and over again. To say that an animal uses it to record the circadian phase at which an event takes place is to say that the stage that the internal process has reached when the event happens is recorded by the animal. The next day when the process has reached that stage again, the animal may expect the event to recur. It might be objected that this is not a kind of temporal thinking at all. All that is happening is that the stage of the oscillation is being recorded, rather than anything specifically temporal. But this would be to miss the point that the oscillator keeps time with the light-dark cycle. That is, the oscillator has its own period, so that if it is kept in constant illumination, it will run at a relatively regular pace, which may be shorte or longer than the ordinary light-dark cycle. But when the animal is exposed to the ordinary light-dark cycle, the oscillator is entrained by it, so that if it is running slower than the light-dark cycle, it will speed up, and if it is running faster than the light-dark cycle, it will slow down. The oscillator is being used to find what time it is, as measured by phase on the light-dark cycle.

We can certainly acknowledge that the animal is representing times, rather than merely possessing a time-dependent memory, that is, a memory whose activation depends on its being in the same phase in the circadian cycle as it was when it recorded the experience, somewhat as the activation of a memory acquired in a drugged state may need the subject to be in that drugged state again. The memory may be used by the animal even at other points in the circadian cycle. For example, the animal may have a memory of food being at a certain place at a certain time. But if the food does not show up at that time, it may continue to check for it at other times, which shows that the memory can be activated at those other times (Gallistel 1990, 245–247).

All that we have so far, though, is a capacity on the part of the animal to record the phases at which particular types of events happen and to put this to use in forming expectations as to what will happen later. We do not yet have any capacity to tell the events of one day apart from the events of another. The base capacity for this discrimination might be provided by including oscillators with a period longer than circadian: the animal could use circalunar or circaannual oscillators, for example. Or the animal might use a decay or accumulation process to differentiate between events at the same phase on different days. But do these methods really give ways of tying down recorded events to particular days? Even if we are considering a system that uses only further oscillators, such as circalunar or circaannual oscillators, there will still come a point at which the system does not differentiate between events that happen at the same phase of the longest oscillator but at different times, for example, events that happen at the summer equinox of different years. This need by no means be a deficiency in the system: the whole point may be that the system is designed to record circaannual phases and has no further interest in putting a date on phenomena. On the other hand, suppose we are considering the use of a decay or accumulation process to differentiate between events that happen at the same circadian phase. Then the system will never confound events that happen at the same phase of some longer-term oscillation. But all we have here is a way of differentiating between events that happen at the same circadian phase on different days. This would be of some use to an animal in remarking, for example, that on days when it was F at one time, it was G at some later time, and that it was G only on those days. There is no need to take the further step of requiring that the animal has a way of recording on which day the event occurred.

There is a dilemma here. When an animal is using a circalunar or circaannual oscillator, we can take it that it really is recording times because of the use to which the recorded information is put when that phase of the circalunar or circaannual oscillator comes around again. This is how the animal's practical grasp of the physical significance of the temporal data operates. But in the very nature of the case, the same factor that makes it so evident that we are here dealing with a record of time also means that we are bound to have the problem of confounding the times of events that happen at different times but at the same phase of the oscillator. The whole point is that the information can be put to use when the same phase comes around again; that is what makes us confident that we are dealing here with a record of time. It might be that we have to think of the animal as counting the number of times at which a particular phenomenon has occurred at a particular phase of the cycle so that it can compute the probability of that phenomenon occurring at that phase of the cycle next time. But all we have here is something of instrumental value to the animal in computing probabilities for future reference, rather than a way of dating past encounters with the phenomenon. On the other hand, suppose we are considering an animal that is using a decay or accumulation process. Here there is no such thing as the phase of the process, if 'phase' is taken to mean a point in an oscillation, for there is no oscillation here at all. This means that there is no problem of confounding events that happen at different times but in the same phase. It also means, however, that there is no prospect of the animal acting on the recorded information when it comes to the same point of the cycle again, just because there is no cycle. So we have no reason to describe the animal as recording which day this or that happened on; all that matters to the animal is that the confound between days has been removed, and merely removing the confound between days does not of itself require that one should have a way of saying which day this or that happened on. The animal's practical grasp of the significance of its use of the decay or accumulation process amounts only to removal of the confound. It might be that the use of the decay or accumulation process does more than simply remove the confound; it might be that in forming its expectations, the animal assigns progressively more weight to what happened on later days rather than on earlier days, for example. So it is not just that there is an existential statement about there having been various days on which various events occurred; the various days are all put in some kind of order by this progressive assigning of order to them. But this in itself does not require that we should yet think of the animal as recording on which day the event happened.

Let us go back to the hypothesis of an animal using an entrained oscillator to record circadian phases. This ability to record the phases of particular happenings enables one to home in on each of several circadian phases as they come around again. But it does nothing to show that one grasps the temporal relations of these phases to one another. More generally, use of a circadian oscillator does not mean that the animal has any conception of the connectedness of time, the fact that every time is temporally related to every other time. The animal has only an ability to reidentify each phase when it appears. And although the animal can in effect use tensed temporal indicators to orient itself with respect to phase, it cannot orient itself with respect to particular times. So it does not have the concept of the past.

If possession and use of a circadian clock is not enough to have the concept of the past, what will do? The traditional answer is an appeal to episodic memory. But it matters how the memories are assigned causal significance. How might they be put to practical use? One use for memory of particular events is in the construction of *scripts* for use next time one encounters an event of that type. For example, when one first has a meal in a prison, one picks up a routine about filing in line, picking up a plate, the pattern of talk and silence, and so on. One might remember exactly what one needed to know for next time—a skeletal script that could be used over and over. But this itself does not put to work the concept of the past, though it does use notions of temporal order and may use the phase of day. As just described, this kind of script formation requires spotting what is relevant for the future as one goes through the procedure. But one might not realize just what is relevant at the time. So there is an advantage in retaining not just a skeletal script of the episode but a rich and circumstantial memory of it. One could then build up a pool of data on which to draw in script construction, and one could return to it for revision in trying to understand what went wrong if a particular script let one down. This pool of data would be exhausted in content by its practical value, by its use as a basis in constructing scripts for future use. It still gives no causal significance to the notion of the particular past times at which the remembered events happened.

How, then, do we give causal meaning to the conception of particular past times? Missing from the types of representation we have considered so far has been any *narrative grasp* of the events recorded, any grasp of the mass of their causal relations to one another. To say this is not to downplay the complexity of the temporal information that can be recorded even by bees with a simple circadian oscillator. They may be recording correlations between phase, food, color, and odor, for example.[1] But this in itself is not enough for the animal to be constructing a narrative from the events in its surroundings. It has no conception of the causal structure of the history of the world around it. What we have just seen, in fact, is that there is no very evident way in which that narrative grasp of the causal structure of the temporally extended world could be a practical grasp.

2.4 An Explicit Physics

Our problem was to find the difference between temporal orientation with respect to phase and temporal orientation with respect to particular time. What we have found is that a creature using a practical physics in interaction with its environment can grasp causal meaning only for temporal orientation with respect to phase. It has no way of putting to work a conception of particular past times. What, then, is needed for a conception of particular times, rather than the phases of some cycle? The fundamental idea needed is that of a process that persists over time and whose later stages causally depend on its earlier ones. Using this idea, one can understand how the way things are at a particular phase of the cycle might causally depend on the way things were the last time the cycle was at that phase. This kind of causal dependence means that the times must be distinct. It need not be a single process that, by connecting two times, distinguishes them. The same effect can be had by considering a chain of interacting processes. In the simplest case, the process has property F at the later time because it was F earlier. A more complex case is when there is an interaction involving the process between the two times. The process may be F when the interaction occurs and, as a result of the interaction, becomes G rather than F. So its later being G depends on its earlier being F. So far we have considered a process that exists at both the later and the earlier times. But when two processes interact, the effects on each may depend in part on the characteristics of the other. So the causal impact of a process's earlier being F may be felt later even if the process that was F has not lasted. (For this notion of *process*, see Salmon 1984, chap. 5.)

The central examples of processes, in the way we actually think about the world around us, are ordinary physical continuants. The later condition of a physical thing depends on its earlier states, together with impacts upon it in the meantime. The fact that we think of physical things as continuously existing and as continuously bearing the marks of earlier interactions over periods means that we can use them to give causal meaning to the continuity of time. This causal connectedness will hold even if there is time without change.

To think in these terms, we need a reflective, or explicit, grasp of the basic physical properties of the objects, such as shape properties, unlike the practical understanding of causally indexical or working concepts that we discussed earlier. We use this explicit grasp of an intuitive physics, not the primitive physics we considered earlier, when thinking of physical objects as internally causally connected over time. My point has to do with the behavior of the object over a period. If an object is spherical, it will roll on an inclined plane, if it is cubical, it will not. If an object is spherical and elastic, it will roll down an inclined plane and may bounce off in one direction at the end. If an object is spherical and brittle, it will roll down an inclined plane and may smash at the end. These examples bring out the point that when we are considering the causal connectedness of an object over time, we often have to consider a family of properties that it has. Bear in mind that in general it is only in conjunction with the other properties the object has that a given property affects its causal powers.

Thinking about the causal dependencies between the states of objects at different times lets us give causal meaning to a rudimentary time ordering of those states. So we can separate the states of objects at different times, though they are at the same phase of the cycle, by the causal relations between them.

It can happen, for example, that one state is the upshot of an earlier one together with an intervening interaction.

Having got this far, we can now use the cycle itself to provide a metric, to give us a way of measuring the intervals between particular times. And this puts further structure on the ordering. Suppose that the causal relations between two events is such that they must have happened on the same day, for example, hearing about Margaret Thatcher's resignation on the radio and hearing about it from a colleague. We can temporally order the two states with respect to each other without considering the direct causal relation between them, by means of the fact that one occurred in the late morning and the other occurred in the early afternoon.

This kind of disengaged understanding of the causal relations between physical objects is, as we saw in the last chapter, exactly what is used in understanding objective, or absolute, space. Suppose that an animal has only a practical understanding of spatial notions, in which the grasp of causal significance is constituted by relations to perception and action, to egocentric space. Then there is no way in which it can achieve a disengaged understanding of time. A creature which has a detached understanding of the causal meaning of temporal notions must have a disengaged grasp of the causal relations among the items in its surroundings, and that is already enough to constitute an objective grasp of the significance of spatial properties and relations. It is not possible to combine a detached or objective understanding of the causal meaning of temporal notions with a purely practical understanding of space.

You may ask whether we really need to exercise a reflective or discursive grasp of basic physical properties in conceiving of objects as internally causally connected. Consider once again Aristotle's artisans, such as the carpenter with his network of working concepts. Surely the carpenter can have an episodic memory of his past encounter with a particular piece of wood, remember how he tackled it and ruefully ponder alternatives he might have tried. Here the idea of the piece of wood as causally connected over time is certainly being put to work, but we are considering someone thinking in practical causal terms. Now in fact, when one has this kind of episodic memory, one will do so against the background of a reflective, or explicit, grasp of other physical properties of the object, such as its shape or weight. But is this necessary? Using an exclusively practical grasp of causation, could one not grasp objects as internally causally connected, and thus after all be using notions of particular past times? This would be very different from the way in which we actually think, but is it impossible? Of course, our actual engagements with particular objects tend to be relatively brief and fragmentary. But the question is whether a purely practical grasp of just the possibility of engaging with the things—the mere potential for such interactions—could not give a creature sufficient grasp of their causal connectedness, and the reach of this possibility is wide. My fundamental point about this way of understanding the causal connectedness of objects is that it is impossible in principle for it to provide one with an understanding of one's own past internal causal connectedness, of the way in which one's past states causally depend on still earlier states one was in. For the whole point about a purely practical grasp of physical properties is that thought of oneself need not be put to use in one's understanding; it is the fact of one's own engagement with the objects that constitutes one's grasp of causal significance. The purely practical level is, ipso facto, a level at which there is no reflective understanding of one's interactions with one's surroundings. There are only the interactions. That being so, at this wholly practical level of thought, there cannot be any understanding of the idea of a range of possibilities in one's past engagements with the things around one, for one is by assumption excluded from having any grasp of the ground of these possibilities. What one needs for such a grasp is a reflective understanding of one's own properties, the properties of things around one, and their causal significance. That is, one needs an explicit grasp of an intuitive physics.

The capacity for temporal orientation with respect to particular time is essential to any narrative understanding of one's own life. If one is to frame any conception of how one will live, one has to have some knowledge of how things have gone so far; plans and projects for the future, a conception of what to do next, cannot be formed in the void. It is not just that we think of ourselves as temporally extended; we think of ourselves as causally structured. We suppose, first, that we are internally causally connected over time, so that one's later states causally depend on one's earlier states: in interaction with the things around one, the way one is after the interaction depends partly on what one was interacting with and partly on the way one was oneself. And, second, we think of ourselves as common causes of correlated sets of effects in the world around us. An understanding of these aspects of one's causal structure evidently demands that one should not just be interacting with one's surroundings but should be capable of reflection on the causal relations between oneself and one's surroundings. It demands understanding and use of the objective spatiotemporal framework as described in chapters 1 and 2. In the next two chapters we will look at the use of the ordinary first person and its relation to self-consciousness and an understanding of one's causal structure. I have first, however, one last set of remarks to make about the past.

2.5   Common Causes and the Time Order

I have talked about assigning causal meaning to the time order and a metric so that we can differentiate between states happening at the same phase of a cycle but at different times. But we also have to understand the significance of saying that one state is earlier and the other later. If we do not give any causal meaning to the distinction between earlier and later, we leave it seeming that in constructing this kind of reflective history of the world around us, we could vary the direction of the time order, the direction from earlier to later, while holding the rest of the story constant. In fact, this is plainly not possible, as we can see by considering a time-reversed film of the ordinary events we observe in a day. What would establish that the film was running backward would be the many correlations that could be explained only in terms of a common destiny toward which they all tended. For example, consider an explosion, with debris flying in all directions. What explains the common velocities of all the bits and the fact that they are all moving away from a single point is the fact of the explosion at that point. In the time-reversed film, the fact that all the bits of debris are moving at the same speed toward a single point would be explained by their coalescence at that point. But in ordinary life we never give such explanations of correlations, in terms of common destiny. The time reversal does not keep our ordinary physics intact. The point here has to do with Reichenbach's *principle of the common cause:* the principle that an antecedently improbable correlation requires explanation in terms of a common cause (1956, 157–167). Reichenbach's thesis of the asymmetry of time was that common causes always antedate the correlations they explain; the correlations are never explained by some subsequent destiny toward which they tend.

What I am proposing here is not, however, a thesis in the philosophy of physics; it is rather that the principle of the common cause is part of the way in which we ordinarily give physical meaning to the temporal order. Part of our understanding of the distinction between past and future is that common causes of a current correlation always lie in the past, rather than in the future. This is not an analytic or unrevisable truth; it is simply part of the way in which we do in fact give a physical interpretation of the temporal order.

The principle of the common cause states that an antecedently improbable correlation between two states of affairs demands explanation in terms of a common cause of the states of affairs. It does not say that there must be such a common cause; only that it is correct to look for one. It is a methodological principle. The obvious application is to the case in which a past event has a number of current consequences. But the principle need not be applied only to uniquely dated events. For example, it is evidently employed in the arguments used to establish Avogadro's number (the number of atoms or molecules in a mole), in which a wide variety of experimental phenomena are all explained by a single value for the number (Salmon 1984). This kind of reasoning also applies to natural kinds: a habitually correlated set of properties, or syndrome, demands explanation in terms of a single underlying cause, a single structural characteristic that explains the several characteristics of the type (Boyd 1979). Some of these atemporal uses of the principle of the common cause seem capable of being grasped and used at the level of practical causal reasoning. One could in that way spot and become acquainted with the characteristics of a particular natural kind, for example. The picture changes when we consider temporal uses of the principle of the common cause. The possibilities here are that a correlated group of phenomena are explained by reference to an earlier common cause and that a correlated group of phenomena are explained by reference to a later joint effect. This latter type of explanation appeals to a teleological explanation of a type generally regarded as incredible. (Of course, this does not count against the familiar types of teleological exploration, which appeal to intention and purpose, for an intention or purpose precedes the various actions it causes.)

You might ask whether animals cannot make use of the conception of past events as common causes of correlated current states of affairs. One approach would be to use the model of thought about the structure of a natural kind as a common cause. For as I remarked, this kind of thinking about common causes seems to be available at the level of practical causal thinking. In the case of a natural kind, we have a subject who encounters a syndrome and develops ever better ways of finding when the trait is present, and separating out relevant from irrelevant aspects of the cluster, in future encounters with the kind. Does this give us a model that we can use in thinking about past common causes? My key point here is that repeated encounters with members or samples of the natural kind is quite possible, so one is constantly reengaging with overlapping examples of the same cluster of symptoms, the same syndrome and there is a great deal of similarity among the various examples one encounters from time to time. Given that a particular thing has some of the features that one provisionally takes to be of diagnostic importance for the kind, one can engage in conjectural hypotheses about what the remaining features of the thing will be. All of this will show up in the complex of ways in which one interacts with the thing.

Does this give us a model for a practical grasp of past common causes for present happenings? Suppose, for example, that one finds puddles in the road in general to be correlated with a rise in the river level. So on a future occasion, when one encounters puddles in the road, one will hypothesize that the river level will have risen, and this may show up in what one does, in the route one takes to cross the river, for example. But that behavior does not show that one has formed a conjecture about a past common cause of the puddles and the river level; it shows only that one has registered the correlation. And we will always be able to do this, to divide through by the assumption that the creature is hypothesizing a past common cause of current events. If a creature only makes the existential hypothesis that there is a common cause for the puddles and the rise in the river level, this can at most entitle it to infer that the correlation will continue in the future. We can always divide through by the existential hypothesis. Only when we have a specific hypothesis—the past cause of the puddles and the rise in the river level was, in particular, rain—is it possible to frame fresh conjectures. Only if we find a subject forming such new conjectures and operating on the assumption that, for example, the freshwater tank will be full, can we begin to suppose that it conceives of a particular past cause of these current states of affairs. Even in this case, it still looks as though we can divide through by the assumption that the subject has a conjecture about a specifically past state of affairs which is the common cause of these phenomena. For all that has happened, after all, is that the subject has formed the hypothesis that there is a lot more water about, without bothering to frame any hypothesis about the particular past cause of this fact. It does not help to consider the case in which the subject comes to recognize that rain will be followed by all these phenomena. This means only what it says: when the subject apprehends rain, it realizes that all these other phenomena will follow. It does not mean that the subject is at any point conceiving of rain as the past common cause of all these phenomena.

Anyhow, the case of rain is quite atypical in that it happens again and again and has its characteristic range of effects every time. Most things that happen are not of this sort. The problem here is that there is a vast diversity in the range of later effects that a past event can have, and none of them need give finely detailed information about the past event. Suppose, for example, that someone blows his nose. This simply does not have any characteristic range of effects, beyond the intended one.

To sum up, our practical thinker could treat rain as a natural kind, a syndrome with a hidden structural cause, but this would give no reason to suppose that the thinker conceived of the particular past event as the common cause of the current correlated phenomena. The point is that whatever pattern of practical reasoning we ascribe to the subject, it seems entirely consistent with it to suppose that the subject has no conception of past times at all but lives entirely in the present and future. The pastness of the hypothesized cause does not seem to show up in the animal's reasoning. All that it recognizes is a syndrome, which may bring with it conjectures as to what else is to be found but no conception of a past state as the common cause.

This point bears on the possibility of empiricist or pragmatist critique of our ordinary ways of representing time. For example, suppose that someone presses hard with such questions as, 'In what does our grasp of temporal notions consist?' The idea behind this question is that all it can amount to is our possession and use of a certain range of ways of interacting with each other and with our environment. In effect, the proponent of this kind of argument takes it that all our grasp of causation can come to is a practical grasp of what to expect in the present and future and having one's actions conditioned by these expectations. If we accept this line of argument, we seem bound to a quite radical reconstrual of our ordinary thought and talk about the past: we are compelled to think of our grasp of the past as exhausted by its implications for present and future perception and action. But if my argument is correct, our grasp of the temporal version of the principle of the common cause cannot in any way be understood in terms of a practical grasp of causation; we have to think of our grasp of the principle as possession of a reflective (or objective or detached) conception of causality. It is certainly legitimate to ask how this reflective understanding of causation and the principle of the common cause is put to work in our thought and talk, but the answer need not take the form supposed by the empiricist or pragmatist. The answer need not take the form of providing a foundation for the social use of language.

The epistemic value of memory—the possibility of its constituting a form of knowledge—may depend on the possibility of sharing memories. Only so, through use of the principle of the common cause to control and correct the use of memory, can one have any reason to think that memory does constitute a form of knowledge. This point depends on supposing that, for memory to constitute knowledge, it is not enough that it "track" the truth, in Nozick's sense (1981, 172–178). It must further not be an accident that in relying on memory, one is relying on a method that tracks the truth; one must be using the method because it tracks. Now we rely on memory because we have evolved to do so, and we have evolved to do so because memory tracks the truth. But we seem to need more than that for knowledge; we seem to need some reason to suppose that the method we are using does indeed track the truth. Descartes's first insight in the *Meditations* is not that certainty is impossible but that we must have some reason, however slight, for thinking that the ways of finding out we actually use really are ways of finding out. Now no attempt to justify our reliance on memory by inductive means can escape an immediate circularity: one must remember particular past results in order to bring induction to bear at all. A more promising approach is to consider our sharing memories. The fact that the general gists of our memories often correspond really does give us, through the principle of the common cause, some reason to think that our memories are indeed accurate. It might be asked whether such use of the principle of the common cause really requires appeal to shared memories, rather than, for example, one's memory of a murder being cross-checked by the bloodstains and the corpse. The main problem with this nonmnemic evidence, though, is its characteristic lack of structure when compared to the richness of memory; my recall of the expression that crossed the victim's face can be matched against your recall of it, but there really seems to be no way of checking this memory against any nonmnemic evidence.

Let me review the course of my argument. I began by asking about the conception of time needed for the conception of oneself as temporally extended. I contrasted a practical grasp of the physical significance of temporal notions with a detached, or reflective, understanding of their physical significance. I looked at some models of a practical grasp of temporal notions and remarked that it seemed unlikely that they could provide a sufficiently rich grasp of time. We seemed to need the ability to use some such principle as the temporal version of the principle of the common cause, but it did not seem possible to have a practical understanding of that principle. Rather, it is used in reflective construction of a narrative of past events, a narrative that makes use of grasp of a shared language. This grasp of the shared language cannot, however, be provided with any foundation of the type sought by empiricists or pragmatists. The conception of time needed to conceive of oneself as temporally extended does not seem to have any foundation at all.

3

The First Person

3.1 Trading on Identity

The question I want to address in this chapter is how we are to characterize the sense of the first person. The notion of the sense of a singular term is due to Frege (1952), who contrasted the sense of a term with its reference, the object for which it stands. It is sometimes held that in the case of the first person, there is no need for the sense of the term. The term 'I' is governed by a simple rule: any token of 'I' refers to whoever produced it. To characterize the meaning of the term, this is all that is needed; there is no need for any further specification of sense. In reply to this it is sometimes said that there must be a much deeper characterization of the meaning of the first person than is provided by the simple rule. For example, it may be held that the rule applies only to uses of the first person in communication and that there is another, deeper use of the first person in soliloquy, where it does express a Fregean sense (Frege 1967). In this chapter I want to consider whether the first person can be said to express a sense, even if the whole story about it is given by the simple rule, and how we might go about characterizing that sense.

To deal with the first person, we need a firm grip on why we need the notion of sense and what constraints there are on a description of sense. In this section I want to consider only this background issue. So suppose that we begin with 'Hesperus' and 'Phosphorus', which are in some ways easier to think about than 'I'. Why do we need the notion of the sense of those terms? They refer to the same thing; why do they not therefore have exactly the same significance? We can see the answer if we consider the following inferences:

Hesperus is F.
Phosphorus is G.
_____
Hence, Hesperus is both F and G.

This inference is not formally valid as it stands. It is en-thymematic, relying upon the suppressed premise 'Hesperus is Phosphorus'. Now, consider what happens if we replace the occurrence of 'Phosphorus' by an occurrence of the coreferential 'Hesperus':

Hesperus is F.
Hesperus is G.
_____
Hence, Hesperus is both F and G.

This inference is really quite different from the first. It is formally valid as it stands. No identity premise is needed, though I have merely substituted one term for another coreferential with it. This second inference trades on the coreferential character of the two uses of 'Hesperus', rather than appealing to any assumption of identity. In contrast, the first inference plainly does depend on the suppressed premise. So there is a sharp difference between 'Hesperus' and 'Phosphorus' in the contributions they make to the inferential roles of the sentences containing them, that is, to what one can infer those sentences from and what one can infer from them. This difference is precisely a difference in sense. Synonymy is that which enables an inference involving two uses of singular terms to trade on their codesignative character, rather than requiring a separate premise to secure it. A description of the sense of a singular term is an account of what would make this trading on identity possible.

The kind of trading on identity with which we are concerned here is not confined to inferences involving conjunctive predicates; any kind of logically complex predicate can be involved. So, for example, we trade on identity when we move from 'Hesperus is F or G' and 'Hesperus is not F' to 'Hesperus is G'. Or again, we contrast the pair 'Hesperus is F' and 'Phosphorus is not F', which is not a contradiction, with the pair 'Hesperus is F' and 'Hesperus is not F', which is a contradiction. It is the introduction and elimination of logically complex predicates in general that brings with it trading on the identities of reference of singular terms, and hence the need for the notion of the sense of a singular term.

It might be objected that the second argument above really is enthymematic but the suppressed premise is an extremely trivial one that we would not ordinarily bother to make explicit. The suppressed premise is simply the logical truth 'Hesperus is Hesperus'. Though trivial, this premise might be held to be needed to link the two uses of 'Hesperus' in the explicit premises of the argument in order to make it formally valid. If this view were correct, we would also need to make sure that the uses of 'Hesperus' in the suppressed premise are linked with the uses of 'Hesperus' in the explicit premises, and we would need further suppressed premises to secure these connections. The problem recurs, and we are embarked on a regress. We have no hope of ever connecting the premises up with the conclusion. If it is valid at all, the second argument is valid as it stands, rather than being enthymematic.

Another line of objection would be to acknowledge that the second argument is valid as it stands but maintain that the first argument is also valid as it stands and does not rely on any suppressed premises. A valid argument, on this view, is one where it is not possible for the premises to be true and the conclusion false. If Hesperus is Phosphorus, then it is necessary that Hesperus is Phosphorus, and this means that it is not possible for Hesperus to be F, Phosphorus to be G, and yet Hesperus to be not both F and G. Now we certainly can define a notion of validity that in this way corresponds with metaphysical possibility, but this is not the notion of validity that is correlative with the notion of sense.

The role that argument plays in our lives is to extend our knowledge, most directly by taking us from knowledge of some truths to knowledge of further truths. We need a notion of validity on which the validity of an argument has some connection with this epistemic role that the argument can play. From this perspective, the crucial difference between the two initial arguments is that in the second inference, someone who knows the premises can, by a simple step, come to know the conclusion without any need to know supplementary premises. In the case of the first argument, knowledge of the two premises on the part of one who does not know that Hesperus is Phosphorus will not, by reasoning alone, take one to knowledge of the conclusion.

The closure of knowledge under known logical implication has become a familiar topic through discussion of Moorean responses to the skeptic such as 'I know I'm in Oxford. I know that if I'm in Oxford, I can't be a brain in a vat on Alpha Centauri. So I know I'm not a brain in a vat on Alpha Centauri.' One may hold the first two of these statements to be correct even while resisting the third. Or again, consider a more everyday type of case: I know that Rosie Lee's is on High Street opposite Merton Street. I know that if Rosie Lee's is on High Street opposite Merton Street, then it is still (even now, since yesterday) on High Street opposite Merton Street. But it is not obvious that I know that Rosie Lee's is still there; I am not really in a position to rule out something's having happened to it since yesterday. This does not seem to undermine my original claim to know where Rosie Lee's is. Such examples bring out the intuitive connection between knowing that *p* and not being easily mistaken about whether *p*. The point about these arguments is that between premises and conclusion there is a shift in what would count as easily getting it wrong, the kinds of circumstances one has to envisage. But these cases do not undermine the connection between validity and the advance of knowledge; it is still true that in cases in which there is not this shift between premises and conclusion, knowledge of the premises, together with correct reasoning, will yield knowledge of the conclusion.

The notion of validity that we need here is the one that logicians have traditionally characterized as formal validity. The second argument above is formally correct as it stands; the first is not. Although 'formal' is the term used in the tradition, it would be wrong to suppose that mere sameness of the shapes of singular terms is what makes it possible for an inference involving them to trade on their coreference. Mere sameness of shape would be quite consistent with the terms involved having quite different references. The reason that the word 'formal' is appropriate is that the notion of validity with which we are concerned is usually captured by formal systems so set up that two uses of singular terms are synonymous just in case they have the same shape or form.

It is sometimes held that a full characterization of the class of valid inferences that concern us can be given without any appeal being made to the notion of sense. To define validity, what we need is the notion of an *interpretation* of a language, that is, an assignment of semantic values to all the primitive nonlogical constants occurring in the language. With this notion of an interpretation explicitly defined, we can proceed to define a logically valid inference as one whose conclusion is true in any interpretation in which the premises are true. There seems to be here no appeal to the notion of sense. So it seems that we can give a full definition of 'semantic consequence' without appealing to the notion of sense. We need only the notions of syntax and reference. This is the view taken by, for example, Michael Dummett (1973). It may be traced back to passages in Frege: "The reference and not the sense of words [is] the essential thing for logic. . . . Logic is not concerned with how thoughts, regardless of truth-value, follow from thoughts. . . . The step from thought to truth-value—more generally, the step from sense to reference—has to be taken. . . . The laws of logic are first and foremost laws in the realm of references and relate only indirectly to sense." [1]

The problem with this line of thought is that it is being applied to formal languages, which are set up so that two signs have the same shape if and only if they have the same sense. The appearance that we can do without the notion of sense is entirely due to this feature of the background, which makes it seem that we can use the notion of sameness of sign without using the notion of sameness of sense. But, of course, that appearance is an illusion. The reason why sameness of sign can do the work allotted to it is that it is sufficient for sameness of sense.

The central point here can be made vivid by considering a language not set up so that sameness of sign guarantees sameness of sense. A plausible example would be a language that contains demonstratives, such as 'that tree'. How are we to go about giving an interpretation for such a language? Do we do it by assigning references to individual words? We can do this only if we individuate "words" more finely than by their shapes or spelling. We have to consider terms, for example, 'that tree', as used in particular ways, for obviously the same demonstrative on different occurrences within a single stretch of reasoning may refer to different things.

What we need is an account of the background constraint on any interpretation of the language, when the interpretation has to assign the same reference to two tokens. The answer is that any legitimate interpretation has to assign the same interpretation to two terms just in case they have the same sense. We cannot do without this background constraint. At best we can mask it by considering only languages in which sameness of sense is guaranteed by sameness of shape or spelling.

The constraint is obscured, even for demonstratives, by formalizations of language with demonstratives, which simply index particular uses of a demonstrative with the reference it has on that use without providing any explanation of how such indexing is to be understood. The idea of such an approach is that the way in which the demonstrative is indexed tells us whether or not an interpretation may legitimately assign different references to two uses of the demonstrative. The rule is that sameness of index requires sameness of assigned referent; difference of index means that different references may be assigned. Suppose, for example, that Old Faithful is a tree and that Woody is a tree. And consider the following inference:

That tree $_{\text{Old Faithful}}$ is F.
That tree $_{\text{Woody}}$ is G.
_____

Hence, that tree $_{\text{Old Faithful}}$ is both F and G.

Suppose now that Old Faithful and Woody are indeed one and the same. Is the inference then valid as it stands? On the face of it, it cannot be. Someone who did not know that Old Faithful and Woody are one and the same but who followed this argument through and as a result of knowing the premises came to believe the conclusion would simply be guilty of a non sequitur. This person would not thereby know the conclusion. But saying that the inference is not valid requires supposing that the indexing being used is not transparent, in W. V. Quine's sense. Otherwise, the inference is valid if Old Faithful and Woody are one and the same. So the indexing is not transparent: sameness of the term used to give the index for two demonstratives means more than merely that they refer to the same thing. If the inference is not valid, then more than actual sameness of reference is required for two uses of the demonstrative 'that tree' to be compulsorily assigned the same reference by any legitimate interpretation of the language. Sameness of indexing is functioning here to indicate that the two uses of the demonstrative involve its being used in one and the same sense, and only that is what makes it compulsory for the interpretation to assign the same reference to both occurrences of the term.

It might be said that the indexing is to be understood as transparent: that sameness of index means no more than that the two occurrences of the demonstrative have the same referent. In that case, if Old Faithful and Woody are one and the same, even though no one ever suspects it, then no legitimate interpretation can assign different references to 'that tree$_{\text{Old Faithful}}$' and 'that tree$_{\text{Woody}}$'. So the argument above has to be reckoned as valid. This notion of validity breaks the connection between argument and the advance of knowledge. Someone who has not the slightest reason to believe that Old Faithful and Woody are the same but who knows that that tree$_{\text{Old Faithful}}$ is F and that tree$_{\text{Woody}}$ is G and concludes from this something is both F and G would have reasoned correctly on this account. But evidently there is no advance in knowledge here, even though his conclusion is correct.

The importance of distinguishing between understanding the indexing as opaque and understanding it as transparent becomes vivid when we contrast perceptual demonstratives with the first person. In the case of perceptual demonstratives, as I have said, we seem to have little choice but to take the indexing to be opaque. In the case of the first person, however, the indexing must be read as transparent. If N.N. argues, 'I am F. I am G. Hence, I am both F and G', then the inference is valid, given only that it was in fact the same person who produced the tokens throughout. There is no further question to be answered before the issue of validity can be decided. This is one of the most striking logical differences between the first person and perceptual demonstratives, and standard treatments of the logic of demonstratives obliterate the point (Kaplan 1989).

As I have been presenting the connection between sense and validity, it has to do with the need to appeal to sense in order to characterize validity. Without the appeal to sense, we cannot guard against fallacies of equivocation. But this does not mean that sameness of sign is a purely superficial phenomenon, and that sameness of sign can ultimately be replaced by an appeal to the notion of sameness of sense. Rather, sameness of sign may often be required for sameness of sense.

Fallacies of equivocation are often of a rather crude kind, such as 'All dogs are male. Some dogs have puppies. So some males give birth.' Here the equivocation on 'dogs' is obvious, and unlikely to fool anyone. But it is a matter of some importance that it is possible to be taken in by fallacies of equivocation. It is entirely possible for a philosopher, for example, to construct, scrutinize and be convinced by an argument that depends on a subtle equivocation in the notion of 'experience', for example. It is simply a mistake to suppose that equivocation is a phenomenon of language only, which could never enter the contents of one's thoughts. Anyone who supposes this has never had it happen to him that he realizes an argument that convinced him did indeed depend on equivocation. And it is a deep fact that we can be taken in by equivocation. In our reasoning we depend on the stability of language, the fact that its signs do not arbitrarily change in meaning from moment to moment. We keep track of the meanings by keeping track of the signs.

3.2   Keeping Track

Before taking up the bearing of these points on first-person thinking, I want to make some further remarks on the implications of taking sense to be correlative with validity in the way proposed.

The norms of argument are among the norms governing our mental lives whose correctness seems to be a priori; even if rational dispute over them is possible, it will be conducted on a priori grounds. Of course, some views see the norms of argument as subject to correction by findings in quantum mechanics, for example, but here I want to set such views aside so as to pinpoint more vividly another way in which the validity of an argument may be not a priori. So consider the principle 'Believe only truths'. Even if this is not quite the right way to formulate it, even if it ought to be elaborated somewhat, the discussion can proceed on the basis of a priori argument. It need not call on assumptions about the character of the environment. In contrast, the way in which this principle is to be applied in particular cases does, in general, depend on how things are in one's environment. Which propositions are true depends, in many cases, on how things are around one.

There is an authentically Cartesian quest for principles governing one's mental life whose correctness, as general principles, can be recognized a priori, and also whose application to one's thinking does not depend on how things are in one's environment. One can recognize by reason and reflection alone how the principle bears on one's cognitive life. Thus, for example, the "clarity and distinctness" of a perception must be recognizable, for Descartes, strictly from within.

Principles governing the validity of arguments may seem to be paradigms of Cartesian norms. One way to put the point is this: Validity applies in the first instance to patterns of inference; it is general forms that are valid or not. And which patterns of inference are valid does not depend at all on the character of one's environment. Whatever one's surroundings, the same patterns of inference are correct. Even if we assume that rational dispute is possible about which patterns are valid, the dispute does not proceed by investigating the world around us. On this approach, whether a given chain of ground-floor reasoning is valid is a secondary matter. It depends on whether it exemplifies a valid pattern of inference. We obtain the distinctively Cartesian conception of inference if we insist that whether a particular ground-floor argument exemplifies a given general pattern is a matter independent of how things are in the thinker's environment.

Let us see how this idea bears on first-person thinking. We can see that there is more to 'I' than its merely having the reference it does by considering the following inferences. Suppose I argue as follows:

I am *F*.

J.C. is *G*.

Hence, I am both *F* and *G*.

This inference is enthymematic. It relies on the suppressed premise 'I am J.C.' Contrast, however, the inference I make when I argue this way:

I am *F*.
I am *G*.

Hence, I am both *F* and *G*.

Here the use of 'J.C.' in the second premise of the first argument has been replaced by a coreferential use of 'I'. This inerence is valid as it stands. It is not enthymematic; there is simply no need for an identity premise. What makes this direct trading on coreference possible is the subject's grasp of the sense of 'I'.

The same point could be made about the logical connections that hold between first-person judgements made at different times. For example, we can contrast the logical relation between 'I am *F*', judged at one time, and the later judgement 'I was *F*' with the nonlogical relation between 'I am *F*', judged at the earlier time, and 'J.C. was *F*', judged at the later time.

In characterizing the sense of the first person, what we now want to understand is how one manages to keep track of oneself through the course of the inference, how can one's grasp of the first person entitle one to conclude that one and the same thing is both *F* and *G*.

The Cartesian conception of inference would demand that whether one is correct in applying the general principle of inference in a particular case does not at all depend on one's relation to one's surroundings. But the Cartesian approach to inference is not at all demanded by the conception of argument as concerned to advance knowledge. All this conception requires is that the general form of reasoning one uses should be correct—and this may indeed be an entirely a priori matter—and that one should have the right to take it that the particular ground-floor argument one is using is indeed of this form. But whether one has this right may indeed depend on one's relation to one's surroundings; it need not be an entirely a priori matter. So even on the conception of argument as concerned to advance knowledge, there is a question about whether we should hold a Cartesian conception of the functioning of the first person in inference.

As a potential model for the use of the first person, let us consider how perceptual demonstratives function in inference, how the ability to keep track of things perceptually relates to our use of perceptual demonstratives in reasoning.

Suppose that one is walking toward a large building. It looks as though it is the same building from moment to moment. But this is not because one is making a series of judgements about it. We have no idea where to begin isolating the brief intervals of perception that one might be thought to be connecting by means of such judgements. It can hardly be supposed that every instant at which one perceives the building is connected to other instantaneous perceptions of it by means of identity judgements; one is not making a continuum of identity judgements in every finite period for which one sees the building. But if we acknowledge that extended periods of perception must be linked by identity judgements, which periods are these? There is obviously no principled answer here; the problem is a fraud.

Of course, there are cases in which one does make judgements of identity on the basis of perception. One may come across a building one does not immediately recognize, and then, from its spatial relations to things one does recognize, conclude that this is an unfamiliar view of a familiar object. But this kind of case of a judgement of identity is not at all like the case under discussion. All that is happening in the case under discussion is that one is walking toward a building, and it is obvious in one's perception of it that it is but a single building over the period of observation. With a bit of an effort, we can tell a science-fiction story in which every time one blinks, the building is annihilated and another one immediately constructed in its stead, by hyperadvanced technology. In this case, one would be making a mistake about identity as one walks along, but the mistake would not be a mistake of judgement.

We can make sense of the idea that the subject might divide the perceptual information he has and suspect that the information on either side of the divide is coming from two different things. In a particular case, one might suspect that though it seems to be the same building, one has actually been taken in by a deceptive feature of the townscape, for example. Raising this question in the everyday kind of case that concerns us is a reflective project. It requires that the subject be thinking about the character of his perceptions. It takes him away from the ground-floor, unreflective use of perception. So long as the subject remains at the level of an unreflective use of perception, there is no point in insisting that he must be using different ways of thinking of the thing from moment to moment, despite the fallibility of his capacity to keep track of the thing.

The point here is to distinguish between the level of perception at which things merely seem to be so, whether or not one actually takes them to be so, and the level of judgement and belief. It is not just that we do in fact take ourselves to be experiencing independently existing things. Rather, perception itself presents things as independently existing; this is just how they seem. This point is frequently remarked, but what does it come to? It involves this: that the subject, in making judgements about particular things, does not divide in his perceptual information concerning them from one moment to the next. The character of perception here, in being perception as of an independent world, consists in part in the way in which perception is related to the level of judgement: one's perceptual judgements about a particular thing are sensitive to one's perception of the thing over a period of time.

In a particular case it is possible for one to reflect on what is happening and to question whether one really has succeeded in keeping track of an object. But this is not the general case. Someone who simply never took himself to be keeping track of objects from instant to instant would be someone for whom perception had ceased to have, as part of its intrinsic character, the representation of objects as independently existing things. Ways of thinking of objects are intrinsically coarse-grained with respect to the underlying perceptual information.

We can sum all this up by considering the following inference:

That building is F.
That building is G.
_____

Hence, that building is both F and G.

Here the two uses of the demonstrative are not anaphorically linked; both involve self-standing uses of demonstratives. Think of the two uses of the demonstrative as separated by a relatively brief interval of time. During this interval there is, or at any rate may be, an interruption in the subject's perception of the building. The subject has no a priori guarantee that one and the same thing is in question. He is not infallible; there is always the possibility of unobserved substitution of one thing for another. Nonetheless, the inference is not enthymematic; the subject has the right to trade on the identity of reference of the two uses of the demonstrative.

This leaves us with a position intermediate between two extreme views. One view breaks the connection between argument and the advance of knowledge and holds that trading on identity is legitimate whenever we have two coreferential singular terms. The other view seeks to respect the connection between argument and the advance of knowledge but supposes that the only way in which this can be achieved is through a Cartesian conception of inference, on which there must be a priori guarantees not only that the form of inference the thinker is using is correct but also that the ground-floor argument in question is indeed of the form the thinker takes it to be. But we can acknowledge the connection between argument and the advance of knowledge without accepting this Cartesian view of knowledge. We can hold that all that is required is that the thinker should have the right to suppose that the argument he is using is indeed of the form he takes it to be. Whether he has that right may depend in part on his relation to his surroundings and the character of those surroundings, and it need not be a matter on which he is infallible. This, of course, is consistent with supposing that the correctness of a general form of inference is an entirely a priori matter. It is also consistent with supposing that the correctness of a general form of inference is to be settled by quantum mechanics, or any other empirical theory.

Can this general picture be employed in the case of the first person? Consider the type of inference with which we began:

I am F.

I am G.

Hence, I am both F and G.

Can we suppose that what we have here is an inference of a valid general form but that there is a fallible skill, the ability to keep track of oneself, that underlies one's grasp of the ground-floor inference itself and licenses one in taking it to be of a correct general form? The proposal here is that the various types of self-knowledge that one has play the same role in relation to the first person as does perception of an object in the case of a perceptual demonstrative. There are many different types of self-knowledge that we have. There is, for example, one's knowledge of the position of one's body, one's knowledge of where one is and what one is doing, one's knowledge of whether one is getting warmer or colder, and so on. All these methods of finding out about oneself give one knowledge of oneself, just as perception of an object gives one knowledge of the object. One might suppose that all these ways of having knowledge of oneself give one a way of keeping track of oneself over time, just as perception of an object gives one a way of keeping track of it over time. The proposal, then, is that when I argue, 'I am F. I am G. Hence, I am both F and G', my grasp of the first person depends on my having a number of methods of self-knowledge that enable me to keep track of myself, so that I do indeed have the right to take my ground-floor argument to have a valid form. If the parallel with perceptual demonstratives really holds, these methods of self-knowledge will give only fallible methods of keeping track of oneself. But as we saw in the case of perceptual demonstratives, that is consistent with the validity of one's argument.

This picture does not ring true for the case of the first person. The obvious way to interpret this idea is that first-person reasoning requires that one should be keeping track of oneself as a physical thing, that one can monitor one's movements as one might monitor the movements of a glass on the table in front of one, and so be sensitive to whether or not another glass is substituted. This is how one has the right to think that there is a single thing in question through the stretch of first-person reasoning. The problem is that this is not a credible description of what goes on. In the first place, one can perfectly well engage in first-person thinking even though one is not in a position to keep track of oneself as a physical object. This is a fundamental point, first observed by Descartes, that any description of the first person must acknowledge and explain. It might be pointed out that even when one is prevented from having this kind of physical self-knowledge—perhaps because one is in a sensory deprivation tank, perhaps simply because one is assailed by skeptical doubt—one still has the capacity for physical self-knowledge. But the mere possession of the capacity cannot explain how one is managing to keep track of oneself. The more fundamental problem is that it is wholly obscure what keeping track of oneself would come to, anyhow. What kind of "unnoticed substitution" for oneself is one looking out for?

The best we can do here is, I think, to consider the following kind of case. Suppose it happens that my sense of balance turns out to be somehow sensitive to your orientation rather than mine, so that when I think 'I am off-balance', it is always you who hits the ground a moment later. Or again, to take a more familiar kind of case, suppose that I am shadowing you through a series of complex movements. All my attention may be on what you are doing, rather than on self-observation. If so, it may happen that I think I am doing X because I see you doing X, but actually my shadowing is rather ineffective, and I am not X-ing at all. So in either case I think 'I am F': that I am off-balance or that I am X-ing. I may also think, correctly, 'I am G', that I am getting older all the time, for instance. And then I draw the conclusion 'I am both F and G'. There is a mistake here, but it cannot be represented as having to do with a failure to keep track of a single thing through the course of the inference. The mistake is in the first premise; the inference itself is unproblematically valid. The first premise identifies the very same person as do the second premise and the conclusion. If there really were such a thing as keeping track of oneself through the course of the inference, then it ought to be possible for the inference to go wrong because of a failure to keep track. But there is no such possibility, so long as the first person is in use. This contrasts with the case of a perceptual demonstrative. It really can happen that, caught in a long line of traffic, I watch the driver of the red Cortina in front of me and remark that he is driving erratically; later, looking at what is in fact a different red Cortina in front of me, I remark that the driver is displaying an Advanced Motorist's badge. When I make the inference, my mistake is due to a failure to keep track of a single thing through the course of the inference. But this cannot happen in the case of the first person.

You might think, then, that the kind of keeping track involved in the case of the first person has to do with a special connection between the first person and psychological predicates. There are two proposals that we have to be careful to distinguish here. One, which when spelled out is evidently unhelpful, is an appeal to a view of self-consciousness somewhat like Berkeley's. One of Berkeley's objections to materialism is that ideas represent by resembling, and an idea can be like nothing but another idea, so ideas cannot represent material substance. Yet according to Berkeley, the self is not an idea either; it is the bearer of one's idea. Yet one can nonetheless think of the self, even though one can form no direct conception of it: one can think of it as the hypothesized bearer of these ideas. So one might try to gloss 'I' as 'the subject of these conscious experiences'. This view evidently does have a serious problem in explaining how it is that one can keep track of the self. If, at one moment, I think 'The subject of these conscious experiences is *F*', and, at another moment, think 'The subject of those conscious experiences is *G*', ostending different sets of experiences on the two occasions, with what right do I take it that the two sets of experiences have same bearer? The problem does not especially have to do with time: it can arise even when I think of the subject of this headache and the subject of that ache. They may be simultaneous experiences, but merely being simultaneous does not guarantee that they will have the same bearer. Of course, what we want to say is that I know them to have the same bearer precisely because I know them to be experiences of mine. But the present approach cannot explain why there is not a simple equivocation in glossing 'I' as 'the subject of this headache' and also glossing it as 'the subject of that ache'. When the first person is used in these different senses, this seems to be simply a verbal shuffle that cannot guarantee that one and the same thing is being referred to. So we should set aside this way of glossing the first person.

An alternative approach is to suppose that the first person functions like a perceptual demonstrative but that psychological properties play the role in the case of this term that physical properties play in the case of a perceptual demonstrative. To be able to identify an object perceptually, one must be able to perceive it and to apprehend at least some of its physical properties, enough to enable one to keep track of it. Similarly, it might be thought, in the case of the first person one has to be linked to the person by self-awareness and must apprehend enough of its psychological properties to enable one to keep track of it. But this position is difficult to sustain. In the first place, psychological properties do not function, as physical properties do, to identify a particular thing: there is no psychological analogue to spatiotemporal location as that which individuates a thing. The best one could do would be to identify a psychological type (Strawson 1959, chap. 4). There is no delineation of an object in psychological introspection; hence Hume's remark about never encountering a self, but only particular perceptions. And in any case, the fundamental problem remains as before: that it is wholly obscure what point the solemn scrutiny of one's psychological properties could be thought to achieve, what unnoticed substitution one might be warily guarding against.

We have seen that perceptual demonstratives do not provide a satisfactory model for the use of the first person in inference. What about proper names? To understand this proposal, we need to know something about the particular model of the functioning of proper names being assumed. On one view, each name is associated with a particular recognitional capacity. Someone who understands 'Hesperus' is able to recognize the planet from its usual position in the sky at night, for example. This sensitivity of one's recognitional capacity to the boundaries of the object is ultimately what enables one to trade on identities in reasoning based on this information. But following through on this model for the first person would involve us in precisely the difficulties we encountered when using the model of perceptual demonstratives. Postulating an ability to recognize one's own boundaries cannot give a way of acknowledging that one trades on identity, in the case of the first person, without depending on any such ability.

This is not, though, the only model we can have for the functioning of a name. Very often the source of knowledge that one expresses using a proper name is not the direct exercise of a recognitional capacity but reliance on testimony: the transmission of knowledge through language, be it by gossip or news broadcasts or whatever. Consider the way in which testimony uses proper names, such as 'Jesse Jackson'. Here we have an individual who is, as it were, radiating information about himself into the community, information transmitted by testimony. Suppose we ask, What is it, for the ordinary hearer, that ties all this information together, as all true of a single individual? One answer would be that on each occasion on which the name is used, the hearer must assure himself by collateral information that the same thing is being talked about. But this would evidently be false to the role that proper names have for us. It is rather the sameness of the name itself that assures us that it is the same thing that is being talked about. Of course, a single name may have different uses, so on occasion, contextual cues have to be supplied to indicate which Jesse Jackson is in question. Or again, consider a historian working in an archive, looking for information about Antonis Mor. It can happen that one finds collateral information about an unnamed individual, on the strength of which one concludes that that individual must be Mor. But the typical case is one in which one finds that the name 'Antonis Mor' itself is used to identify the person. And that itself is enough to produce the presumption that the same person one already has information about is being written about here too. One pools together various pieces of information in the archive, as all true of a single person, because the same name is being used. Without proper names, the dissemination of testimony in our community would be a relatively disorganized matter. What ties the testimony into bundles, what organizes it into usable clusters, is our use of the names themselves. Grasp of a proper name thus provides a way of being presented with an object, a way that would not be available if one did not grasp the name; grasp of a proper name genuinely expands one's conceptual repertoire. Sameness of proper name can have an ineliminable role to play in making it legitimate to trade on an identity. So which proper name is being used is a matter that enters directly into the inferential role of a piece of knowledge.

Can we use this model of the functioning of proper names to illuminate the way in which the first person operates in soliloquy? The problem with the model emerges when we reflect that testimony is an indirect mode of knowledge, in the following sense: knowledge obtained through testimony must ultimately derive from knowledge obtained otherwise than on the basis of testimony. And if we ask why it is legitimate to suppose that the use of proper names really does organize testimony into bundles of information all true of single things, the underlying justification is that the primary sources of the testimony disseminated throughout the community are using their perceptual capacities to distinguish individual objects. But there is no such underlying justification in the case of the first person. There is simply the fact that all one's modes of self-knowledge represent themselves as giving one information about oneself. And these modes of knowledge are not indirect in the sense in which testimony is indirect. The information does not derive from some underlying level at which the information is in some more basic way all sorted as true of a single thing. So this model does not seem to function any better as a model for the operation of the first person.

It might be wondered whether the lack of any need to keep track of oneself is not somehow a rather superficial phenomenon, whether it is not somehow an artifact of the way in which the situation is described, as a case in which it is indeed one and the same thinker that we are considering over a period, so that it is built into the description that no error can be made. In a sense that is right; the phenomenon is related to this description of the situation. But it is by no means a superficial matter that this is the right way to describe the situation when we are considering questions about sense and reference.

Notice to begin with that this way of putting things presupposes that what fixes the reference of the first person is the simple rule that any token of 'I' refers to whoever produced it. Only through this rule does the mere fact that we are describing a single thinker over a period of time guarantee that his use of 'I' keeps track of a single thing. So the model of the perceptual demonstrative, which is not governed by any rule, must be set aside. As we will see, this is not an easy matter. There is persistent pressure to suppose that the rule of reference for 'I' cannot be the whole story about the way in which the reference of the first person is fixed, that something like the model of the perceptual demonstrative must come back into play when we consider the relation of the first person to self-consciousness.

Furthermore, notice that there are cases in which we can find some semblance of a failure to keep track of a single self, even though these cases are wildly counterfactual as things stand. Such cases are quite radical, and it is best to state one by considering a species quite different from our own.

Suppose, then, that we have a creature that, though intelligent, is like the amoeba in that it frequently fissions and like some types of particles in that it frequently undergoes fusion. In fission, the products of the fission both inherit all the psychological properties of the original. In fusion, as much as possible of the psychological lives of the originals are passed on to the successor; we may suppose that fusion only occurs between individuals that have a lot in common to begin with. It is often said that were fission or fusion widespread, the ordinary notion of a person would be inapplicable. My discussion here lets me pinpoint why this is so. The point is that the creatures involved in fission and fusion could have nothing like our ordinary use of the first person. A creature which found itself with the thoughts 'I am *F*' and 'I am *G*', would have no right whatever to suppose that it was one and the same thing that was *F* and *G*. These thoughts might have come from different participants in the fusion that produced the creature, or an ancestor of it. And a creature that found itself with the thought 'I was *F*' would have no reason to suppose that the thing that was *F* is the same as what it can now directly tell to be hungry. For it might have the thought 'I was *F*' only as the result of an earlier fissioning, and being *F* might be a property of the original rather than of any of its successors. The world of these creatures is simply not able to sustain our ordinary use of the first person in thinking and reasoning. They cannot have the first person. For this reason, they are not persons.

What is less often noted is that the ordinary notions of belief and desire also find only attenuated applicability to such creatures. There are norms of rationality that we aim to conform to in our thinking, in however rudimentary and unsatisfactory a way. There must be some semblance of rationality if we are to have beliefs and desires at all. But these norms of rationality are intrapersonal. There is a problem in my thinking if I find myself believing one thing and also impelled to believe its contrary. If I am rational and understand the situation, I have to recognize that this is unsatisfactory. It is quite a different matter if I find that while I believe one thing, someone else believes something incompatible with it. It is not unreasonable to regard this as a matter of indifference, barring some reason to give weight to the other person's view. I can plan my actions on the basis of my own belief without having to wonder about his. In contrast, if I find that I hold contradictory beliefs, I simply cannot rationally regard this as a matter of indifference when planning my actions. This brings out something of the sense in which the canons of rationality are intrapersonal. They oblige me to keep my own house in order; they do not oblige me to make it just like everyone else's. For creatures that are continually fissioning and fusioning, however, a cognitive economy cannot run in this way. The psychological life of an individual is too closely tied to those of earlier ancestors that fissioned or fused, and later successors into which it fissions or with which it fuses for it to be possible to give any special weight to the internal organization of a single short-term psychological life.

These points bring out that fact that our ordinary use of the first person, and the way in which we trade on identities in inferences involving it, does indeed depend on contingencies about the way the world is. And they suggest that this is not an isolated point about the first person. The whole structure of the way in which we think about belief-desire psychology depends on this psychology's being organized as the life of a self-conscious person.

It is important to observe that these points relate only to the radical case of a species that frequently and pervasively fissions and fuses. We cannot obtain any of these conclusions simply by considering a case in which a first-person memory is transplanted from one person to another, so that the second person seems to remember doing what the first person did. There is no failure to keep track here. For whose failure would it be? So long as the first person has the memory, it is indeed a first-person memory relating to what he himself did. At no point does he lose track. When the second person acquires the seeming memory, he simply acquires a false belief about what he himself did. At no point does he have to keep track of who is in question; at no point does he lose track of who is in question.

So the possibility of a species of the type I indicated, radically different from us, does not show that we have to keep track of ourselves in order to ensure that we are not in that situation. In fact, we are not in that situation, and this gives us the right to use the first person as we do. In using the first person in inference, trading on identities involving it, one is not relying on a fallible capacity to keep track of oneself. Nonetheless, what gives one the right to take these inferences to be of valid forms is not something given purely a priori; it is the background contingency that we are in fact creatures whose psychological lives preserve their integrity over extended periods.

There is an analogy that, I think, helps in characterizing the contingency on which our use of the first person depends. Suppose that you are looking at a set of video screens, each of which is showing a somewhat different scene being relayed by a distant camera. You have the problem of piecing together the total situation from all these images over time. This means that you have to identify objects from screen to screen and within a particular screen over time. For example, something that shows up as large, irregular, and rusty on one screen ought also to show up as large, irregular, and rusty on the other screens in which it appears. And it ought to retain a certain stability in the way it appears over time on any one screen. The problem of object-identification here, and the way in which it is solved, is parallel to the problem that we have in perception of identifying objects perceived through different sensory modalities or within a sensory modality over time. We have to use the content of the information we receive about the objects to tell us whether it is the same thing that is in question. And it is quite possible that while the information we receive about two objects is individually accurate, we make a mistake in identifying them.

There is another case we should look at. Consider the problem of finding out whether the various scenes shown by the video monitors are all happening at the same time. One way to proceed would be exactly as before: to use the internal evidence of the information provided by the screens to establish whether it is plausible that all these happenings are simultaneous. It would be quite possible that while information provided by two screens was accurate one went wrong in supposing that it was all happening at one and the same time. There is, though, another possibility, which stands out clearly if we forget about the possibility of recording the scenes shown and suppose ourselves to be dealing with a closed-circuit TV system. In this case, there will be no need to use the internal evidence of the information provided to weigh up whether the scenes shown are all happening simultaneously. One simply uses the brute fact that they are all being shown simultaneously. If the information they provide is accurate, then one cannot go wrong in supposing that they all concern one and the same time. Our perceptual systems may well operate in this way, taking it that information obtained through different perceptual systems relates to the same time not because of the causal coherence of the detailed narrative one could thereby construct but rather because of the brute fact that the different perceptual systems all produced their various pieces of information at the same time.

Consider now the use of the first person in stating the content of the various pieces of information that we have about ourselves: where we are, the positions of our limbs, our past lives, our emotional states, and so on. How does one know that all the first-person knowledge one has, obtained in all these different ways, concerns a single thing? As we have seen, one answer would be that one uses the internal evidence of the information obtained in all these various ways to find whether one can coherently put it together as a narrative all true of a single thing. But this is not a credible description of how we proceed. An alternative approach is to suppose that the way in which we operate is, rather, analogous to the way in which judgements about time might function. We exploit some fact about the whole system, for example, that scenes whose showings are simultaneous are themselves simultaneous or else that the various perceptual systems are all wired together as the systems of a single animal. On this model, there is no need to use the specific contents of the information one has to ensure that it is a single thing that is in question. The model of keeping track of an object across the video screens would be quite inappropriate.

3.3 The First Person as a Token-Reflexive

At the level of a description of our use of language, we want to know what gives one the right to take the different tokens of 'I' one produces to refer to the same thing. As we have seen, no model that assimilates 'I' to a perceptual demonstrative or a proper name seems promising here: there is no keeping track of an object. A better proposal is that some relation among the tokens of 'I' themselves is what gives one the right to suppose that they all refer to the same thing.

This is exactly the result secured by viewing 'I' as a token-reflexive, that is, as governed by a rule that identifies the reference of any token of 'I' as the thing that bears some relation to that token. The specific rule here is the following:

Token-reflexive rule   Any token of 'I' refers to whoever produced it.

The fact that two tokens are governed by this rule and the fact that they were produced by the same person are enough to guarantee that inferences by this person that trade on the identity of reference of the tokens are legitimate. There is no possibility of a person referring to himself twice using the first person but associating different senses with it on both occasions.

A similar approach might be proposed for 'now'. This term is governed by the rule that any token of it refers to the time at which it was produced. So what makes trading on identity legitimate in an inference involving uses of 'now' is a relation between the tokens themselves: that they were produced at the same time.

We still have to understand how this can be correct, though, for the point does not seem to hold good for token-reflexive terms in general. For example, consider the case of 'here'. We can take 'here' to be governed by the rule that any token of it refers to the place where the speaker is. But it does not follow from this that it is valid to trade on the identity of any two tokens governed by this rule that are in fact uttered at the same place. It is entirely possible that the speaker may take himself to have moved between the utterance of the first token and the utterance of the second, even though he has not. In this case, the trading on identity is not valid, even though both tokens are governed by the rule and were in fact produced in the same place. It might be replied that we ought to consider the case in which the two tokens of 'here' are produced simultaneously, or at least that we abstract from the effects of a time difference between them. This would place the treatment of 'here' on a par with the treatment of 'now' proposed above. Even under this restriction, though, there remains a difference between 'here' on the one hand and 'I' and 'now' on the other. The relation among tokens of 'here' that we have to consider as generating sameness of reference is that of their having been produced in the same place. And this relation does not seem to be immediately given to the subject in the way in which the simultaneity of two tokens or their having both been produced by the subject is immediately given. The knowledge that two tokens of 'here' were produced at the same place is, in this kind of case, a product of the realization that the tokens of 'here' were produced simultaneously by the same person and that a single person cannot be in two different places at the same time.

What this line of thought suggests is that what gives one the right to trade on the identity of reference of two tokens of 'I' is the fact that one knows that one produced both tokens. This cannot be quite the right way to put it, though. It suggests that what is doing the work is the reasoning 'I produced this token of "I". I produced that token of "I". Hence, both tokens were produced by the same person.' And then we would have to ask what made *this* trading on identity legitimate. We need a notion of the thinker's being sensitive to the fact that he did produce both tokens of 'I' where this fact is not mediated by his having the thought 'I produced both tokens of "I" '. But this notion of sensitivity to the fact of coproduction seems, once we reflect on it, to give way to a further point.

Suppose we ask what the 'sensitivity to coproduction' is supposed to guard against. What would it be for one not to be sensitive to the fact of coproduction? The case would have to be one in which I am not sensitive to whether two tokens of the first person were in fact both produced by me, as opposed to its happening that one was produced by me and another was produced by someone else. So, for example, it might happen that I say 'I am F', someone else says, 'I am G', and I conclude, 'I am both F and G'. This would be a case in which I am not sensitive to whether the two tokens are coproduced by me. But let us consider the case more slowly. Can we really say that there is a mistake of inference here, that I have grasped propositions that individually may each be correct and that the mistake has come only at the inference step? This, after all, is what characteristically happens when an inference depends on equivocation. The premises are individually correct; the mistake comes only when an inference is made that would be valid only if the two uses of an expression had the same sense, and they do not. But in the case we are considering, are the premises each individually correct? I say 'I am F'; this, we may suppose, is all right. Someone else says, 'I am G', and this too, we suppose, is correct. And then I make the move to 'I am both F and G', and this, we assume, is not correct. But is the mistake here a mistake of inference? It must be that I move to the conclusion only because as well as my saying, 'I am F' the other person said, 'I am G'. Unless we have the causation here, we do not have anything recognizable as an inference. But the mere fact of causation is not enough to make this an inference; I must not only have been somehow causally affected by the other person's utterance but must also have made something of it. And now the question is what exactly I made of that utterance. One possibility is this: I said 'I am F'. Then I heard the other person's utterance, and I thought 'Aha! So that person is G'. And then I moved to the conclusion. In this case, there was a mistake of inference, but not through a failure to be sensitive to whether tokens of 'I' were being coproduced. What happened was rather an almost incredible non sequitur. Alternatively, it might be that I simply echoed, or shadowed, the other person's utterance and thought 'I am *G*'. In this case, there was no mistake in the inference. The problem lies rather in the second premise, where I foolishly echoed the other person's utterance and took the result on board, so to speak. And this can happen.

What this brings out is a background assumption of this whole inquiry into sense, which I have not so far made explicit, namely, that we are considering a single subject engaged in inference and that for an inference to be made, we must have a single subject who simultaneously grasps the premises and conclusion of the inferential step. For an argument to be formulated at all, we require a single subject to orchestrate it; we cannot have the various premises and conclusion distributed across different subjects, with no one marshaling them all together. This is true of any inference, not just those involving the first person. This background point about inference—that it is engaged in by a single subject—explains why it is legitimate for a subject to trade on the identity of any two tokens of 'I' that he has himself produced. It is still true that the only aspect of the meaning of 'I' to which we have to appeal here is that it is governed by the token-reflexive rule. The conclusion I reached earlier is reinforced: we do not need any further conception of the way in which the self is displayed to the subject.

You might have wondered earlier whether I am not making excessive demands on the token-reflexive rule. The relation between the rule of reference for a singular term and the inferential role of that term is, after all, open to dispute. I have been proceeding as if it must be possible to derive the inferential role of a singular term from a statement of the reference rule for it. That is what led me to suppose that it must be the thinker's sensitivity to whether the tokens were coproduced that licenses his trading on identity in inferences involving them. But, it might be said, the norms governing the inferential role of the tokens—whether it is legitimate to trade on identity in inferences involving them—are actually more fundamental than the norms governing the determination of reference, so the whole project was misconceived.

This overstates the case. It may indeed be that the norms governing inferential role are more fundamental than, or at least as fundamental as, the norms governing the determination of reference. But this does not mean that the norms of inference are in no way responsible to the way in which reference is determined. Consider, for example, a community of war criminals, who all have first-person memories of committing atrocities. They may refuse to trade on identity in weaving these memories in with their thoughts about their present lives. (In effect, they treat those memories as being Q memories [quasi memories], in the sense of Shoemaker 1984b, that is, they derive from experiences of past events, but not necessarily their own experiences of those past events.) Now if the norms governing inference were genuinely more fundamental than, and in no way responsible to, the norms governing the determination of reference, then there would be nothing we could say to such people. They have their norms, and we have ours, and there seems to be no place for rational dispute. This picture changes once we realize that the norms governing inference have to be comprehensible in the light of a reference rule for the first person. What makes rational dispute with these criminals possible is that they, like us, recognize that their use of the first person is governed by the token-reflexive rule, and this means that the dispute can be organized around the question of when we do and when we do not have the same person again. And to this question many considerations are relevant.

We have been concerned with the broad outlines of the point of contact between the rule of reference for the first person and the norms of inference governing it. We have seen that we need not bring them into harmony by supposing the subject to be sensitive to the coproduction of two tokens of 'I'; rather, we are dealing here with a background assumption of the whole inquiry into sense and the way in which this assumption interacts with the token-reflexive rule.

This point is not peculiar to my approach to the notion of sense. It also applies to Frege's way of introducing the notion, in terms of cognitive significance. Frege too considers judgements made by a single subject and the question of the informativeness of particular judgements for that subject. So for Frege too, the fact that the first person is governed by the token-reflexive rule means that the subject's judgement 'I am me' is never informative, not because the subject is sensitive to the fact that the tokens are both being produced by the same person, but because the question does not arise whether it is the same person twice: in all the subject's thinking there is no possibility of him using 'I' on different occasions to refer to different things.

Finally, consider the case in which one hears someone else state 'I am F' and 'I am G' and concludes that one and the same person is both F and G. In this case, one would ordinarily proceed by using one's knowledge of who produced both statements, that it was 'that woman', for example. But I think we can imagine cases in which the inference might proceed in a way where the idea of being sensitive to coproduction might actually find some application. Suppose, for example, that one is listening to a number of voices simultaneously over a long period, all of which are making first-person statements. And suppose that one is listening simply for whether any one of these people makes a particular conjunction of self-ascriptions. It might then happen that one recognizes that someone has

been said to be both *F* and *G*, without having consciously identified either who is said to be *F* or who is said to be *G*. This
would be a case in which the model of being sensitive to coproduction really does apply. There would, of course, be a possibility of error in this case, and there would be evident
restrictions in the kind and quantity of information one could
know to be true of anyone there, in contrast to the mass of
information that one ordinarily has about oneself.

4

Self-Reference and Self-Knowledge

4.1 The Problem

The problem that concerns us now is the relation between, on the one hand, the way in which the reference of the first person is fixed and, on the other hand, both the bases on which we make first-person judgements and the consequences we draw from such judgements. This is a special case of the problem of the relation between the way in which the reference of a singular term is fixed and the ways in which we go about verifying judgements that use the term and drawing the implications of such judgements. This in turn is a special case of the problem of the relation between the ascription of a semantic value to a term and its conceptual role, which consists of both the bases on which we make judgements involving the term and the consequences we draw from those judgements. The most familiar form of this very general issue is the relation between the ascription of semantic value to a logical constant and the inference rules for it.

Our thinking about this problem in the case of the first person tends, as we have seen, to be dominated by the model of perceptual demonstratives, terms such as 'that man' used to indicate someone currently seen, for example. In the case of a demonstrative like this, the reference of the term seems to be fixed by a causal link; I can't refer, in that way, to a man to whom I am not causally linked. This causal link also seems to have a lot to do with the bases for judgements about 'that man' and the consequences that we draw from such judgements. The causal link here that fixes the reference is also a perceptual link. So relying on the link gives me a basis on which I can make judgements using the term 'that man'. Moreover, the perceptual link can also guide my actions. So I can use it in finding the pragmatic implications, the implications for my own actions, of my judgements about 'that man'.

On this model, it seems that we can take the referential link to be fundamental and derive from it the correctness of the conceptual role that we ordinarily ascribe to the term, the use we make of it. The referential link, as well as being a referential link, in effect gives a specification of the ways in which the term can be used. So perceptual demonstratives here stand in contrast to the first person. The reference of the first person seems to be fully characterized by the token-reflexive rule. To repeat, this rule says that any token of the first person refers to whoever produced it. This gives an invariably accurate statement of the reference of any token of 'I'. The contribution of the first person to the truth or falsity of any statement in which it appears has been fixed. There has been an appeal to a causal relation: the referent is the person who produced that token of 'I'. The referential link is production of the token. But that causal relation does not seem to be an epistemic relation. It does not provide one with a way of finding either the bases for making first-person judgements or the consequences that one draws from those judgements. So this case is in sharp contrast to the case of a perceptual demonstrative.

The notion of the producer of a token is not straightforward. There may be many people causally involved in the production of a token: torturers and interrogators and so forth. And it would not be enough to say that *the* producer of a token is the person whose vocal chords were used in producing it, for someone whose own vocal chords had been cut might be equipped with a device to enable him to make use, on occasion, of someone else's vocal chords in communication. And perhaps a really deep analysis of the notion we need here would show it to have some epistemic aspect: perhaps *production* of a token in the sense we need has to do with one's being causally related to the token in such a way that it can be used to communicate or express knowledge that one has. But for our my purposes, the important point is that I am not using the notion of the producer of a token in a quite special sense in connection with the first person. If someone produces a token of 'that man', this relation of production is not itself an epistemic relation to the referent of the term. Just so, if someone produces a token of 'I', this relation of production is not itself an epistemic relation to the referent of the term. But in the case of 'I', it is this relation of production that fixes the reference of the individual token. So there is indeed a contrast here with the case of perceptual demonstratives.

I can make this vivid by asking you to suppose a people who, though intelligent and possessed of a shared language, nonetheless have no use for the first person. They have no such sign in their language. And perhaps they also fail rudimentary behavioral tests for self-consciousness. We can say to them that they ought to consider introducing the term 'Id' into their language, which should be governed by the rule that any token of it refers to whoever produced it. And they might indeed fall in with this proposal. They might introduce the term and stipulate that it is governed by that rule. But this of itself will not render them self-conscious. The modes of self-knowledge that we have might still be a mystery to them.

It is not that they would have no use whatsoever for 'Id', but whatever use they do have would be severely circumscribed. The bare statement of the token-reflexive rule does not leave one entirely in the dark about how the use of the term might express knowledge. For one can, on occasion, find out something about the producer of a token from the mere fact of his producing it. For example, if the token is produced with a note of alarm, one might say, 'Whoever produced that token of "Id" sounded alarmed'. So if the person had said 'Id is alarmed', one might then judge his statement to be true. Yet it is harder to see how one might go about using the term oneself to make knowledgeable judgements. Presumably, one would need a scenario in which all of the following conditions were met: one could find out something about the person merely from his producing the token, for example, that he was alarmed; the producer of this token of 'Id' was in fact oneself; and one expressed the knowledge obtained from one's merely producing the token, the knowledge of alarm, for example, by immediately appending a predicate to this token of 'Id'. This would be a bit like completing someone else's sentence for him. In this case, the "someone else" would actually be oneself, but one would not realize this, since, *ex hypothesi,* one is not self-conscious and has no conception of oneself. This would be a rather unusual case, and I mention it only to bring out just how limited a grasp the token-reflexive rule, of itself, gives us on how we might go about using the first person in knowledgeable judgements.

Even if one does manage to use a the term 'Id', governed by the token-reflexive rule, to express knowledge in this rather strained way, the knowledge would still not be an exercise of self-consciousness. Even if one did manage to compile the statement 'Id is alarmed', there would still be the question, 'But was it I who produced that token of "Id"?' Of course, for most of us, the answers to such questions are ordinarily obvious. I may know that it was I who produced the token simply because I produced it intentionally. One use of the ordinary first person is to express such agent's knowledge. But we have, so far, no way of explaining how a term governed by the token-reflexive rule can be used to express such knowledge. All that we have is the ability to find characteristics of the producer of the token from his producing it.

Someone might point out that we can imagine a use of singular terms that stands to our ordinary use of perceptual demonstratives somewhat as the use of 'Id' stands to our ordinary use of the first person. Suppose that we have a community that does not use perceptual demonstratives. They may have ordinary proper names and other referential devices, such as definite descriptions, but they do not use terms such as 'that man' in the way in which we do. We might propose to these people that they should introduce terms of the form 'that *F*', functioning in such a way that any use of the term 'that *F*' refers to the thing that caused the production of that token. And we might lay down quite stringent and explicit conditions on the kind of causal link in question, so that it really is just the kind of causal link that matters to us in our use of perceptual demonstratives. And these people might accept our proposal and make the suggested stipulation. They are not yet, however, in much better a situation than our hypothetical users of 'Id'. Given a particular token of 'that *F*', they might on occasion be able to find out something about the thing that caused production of the token, from the mere fact of its causing production of the token. So they might be able to go in for some very limited assessment of each others' uses of the term. And by "completing their own sentences," they might be able to make some very limited uses of the terms themselves. But this impoverished repertoire is not even a fragment of our ordinary use of perceptual demonstratives. The key point is that so far, they might simply not realize that the term with the reference rule they have explicitly characterized can actually be used to report the unreflective deliverances of perception, to say what they see, for example. The difference that is doing the work here is the difference between using the term according to a fundamental reference rule laid down by explicit stipulation and using in such a way that it is governed by that same reference rule, but not as a result of explicit stipulation. We might also apply this contrast to the case of the users of 'Id'. They do indeed take the token-reflexive rule as the fundamental rule governing 'Id', but only by explicit stipulation. The thesis is still in play that any community that uses 'I' in such a way that the fundamental rule governing it is the token-reflexive rule, but not as a result of explicit stipulation, must be using 'I' in a way that is apt for expressing self-knowledge. The problem is still to see why this should be, what the connection is between the use of a term subject to that rule and our characteristic modes of self-knowledge.

In the case of a perceptual demonstrative, the causal link that fixes the reference of the term also yields knowledge of the thing referred to and can guide one's actions with respect to it. So if that causal link is fixing the reference of the term otherwise than through explicit stipulation, it is still apparent how the reference of the term is related to its having the conceptual role that it does. In the case of the first person, however, if we suppose that the production link between the person and the token is what fixes the reference of the token and that this is secured otherwise than through explicit stipulation, we still have to bear in mind that this production link does not in general provide one with any knowledge of the reference of the term.

It might be said that there is simply no problem here: the determination of reference is one thing, and the conceptual role of the term is another. There may be no intelligible relation between them. This is the traditional stance of the uncompromising realist. Setting the truth conditions of our statements is one thing, and the bases on which we can claim to know their truth and the consequences we can draw from them are another. In general, this position is helpless before a skeptical challenge, and it is so here. It leaves open the possibility of someone who uses the first person in compliance with the token-reflexive rule, and not because of an explicit stipulation, but who is skeptical about whether any of the customary methods of finding out about oneself really do yield knowledge expressible in the first person. This person, even though he is not a skeptic about the external world, would dispute that perception ever yields any knowledge about one's own characteristics. He would dispute whether his sense of bodily position ever yields any knowledge of his own bodily position, and he would dispute whether he ever has any knowledge of psychological states expressible in the first person. Of course, such a person would be out of touch with his own feelings but the case actually seems to be even worse, if such a thing is possible. It is hard to rest with a position on which such skepticism is tenable. It is just as hard as it would be to rest with a view on which the semantic value of a logical constant and the inference rules governing it have no bearing on one another.

The problem I have identified is to find the relation between the rule of reference for the first person and the various ways that we have of finding out about ourselves. We can pursue the problem by considering the self-knowledge provided by vision. Vision provides knowledge of one's own movements on the basis of what Gibson (1986, 118–123) called the flow of the optic array. The focus of expansion of the array is the direction in which one is going; the focus of contraction of the array is the direction from which one is coming. The rate of one's movement is specified by the rate of flow. Of course, the flow pattern can shift as one changes direction or speed, though in a stable environment there will be no concomitant shift in the underlying "invariants of structure and texture": they "specify the unmoving terrain, whereas the flow pattern specifies the observer's locomotion with respect to the terrain." As Gibson points out, the optical flow is almost never experienced as movement of the things around one; it is simply *"experienced as kinesthesis, that is egolocomotion."* Another aspect of visual proprioception is its use to register turning and tilting of the head. In the vestibule of the middle ear there are three pairs of semicircular canals set in place relative to the three axes of head rotation; they register turns and tilts, specifying the degree of rotation. But head turns and tilts are also registered by vision. They are registered by the sweeping of the field of view over the ambient array during head turns and the wheeling of the field of view over the array during head tilts. This again gives one knowledge immediately expressible in the first person, though one may take a little practice in articulating such judgements as 'My head is tilted to the right', 'My head is turning slowly to the left and tilting up'. Finally, there is perhaps the most obvious type of visual proprioception: sight of one's own body. This plays a central role in visually guided action, such as visually guided hand movements, including manipulation and tool using. Sight of one's own body also tells one about the contact of one's extended limbs with surfaces. "When the decreasing occlusion of the surface by the extremity ceases, and when there is no accretion of deletion of surface texture by the occluding edges of hand or foot, then the extremity is in contact with the surface and not sliding over it. This specifies, for example, that the foot is on the ground." Since terrestrial animals usually have both feet on the ground and have not just tactile but also visual information about this, we can understand why human infants and other terrestrial animals are distressed by being on an invisible glass floor high above the real floor. And, of course, sight of one's own body yields a flood of information that can be directly articulated in the first person.

The question we now have to address is how this information can indeed be directly articulated in the first person, how a term governed by the token-reflexive rule can be used to express the knowledge of oneself made available by visual proprioception. One obvious response is to balk at the difficulty of the problem so stated and to suppose that there is another use of the first person than the one on which it is governed by the token-reflexive rule. So one might, with Frege (1967), distinguish between the 'I' of communication and the 'I' of soliloquy and suppose that only the 'I' of communication is governed by the token-reflexive rule. The use of the first person in soliloquy is what directly expresses the self-knowledge made available by visual proprioception, and this use of the first person is not governed by the token-reflexive rule. In this use, the first person functions more like a perceptual demonstrative. As we saw in chapter 3, this move is perennially appealing, but it does not ultimately satisfy. We have to acknowledge that there is no use of the first person on which it is not governed by the token-reflexive rule, and we have to abandon the perceptual model of self-consciousness. Even in the case of perceptual self-knowledge, the character of the self-knowledge cannot be modeled on perception of other objects. And abandoning the perceptual model of self-consciousness ultimately means abandoning the view of 'I' as a perceptual demonstrative.

So the problem remains: we have to explain how a term governed by the token-reflexive rule can be used to give the most direct articulation of the knowledge made available by visual proprioception. Now another proposal would be that visual proprioception already uses the first person. Since a term governed by the token-reflexive rule already figures in the content of the perception itself, there is no difficulty about why the first person should be capable of giving direct articulation to the knowledge provided by the perception. The problem is analogous to the question why the notion of a tree should be capable of figuring in direct reports of the knowledge made available by perception. The obvious answer is that things sometimes are visibly trees; the perceptual system itself classified them as trees. Since the concept figures in the content of the perceptions themselves, there is no special difficulty about how it can also figure in the reports of what is known on the basis of these perceptions.

There is, indeed, a problem about how the term governed by the token-reflexive rule, and said to figure in the contents of the perceptions really can be uncritically taken to refer to the same thing as does the perceiver's use of 'I'. In the first place, there is no term literally showing up in one's perceptions at all; it is not as if vision is subtitled. But perhaps we can accommodate this fact by speaking of token concepts, which figure in vision and are governed by the rule that any token of this type refers to whoever produced it. A further problem is that the token is not literally produced by the person himself. It is not up to us what we see. Of course, we can decide where and whether to look, but what we see when we do so is not always under our control, and one can see oneself to be somewhere one did not expect to be, and rather hoped one would never be. It is the perceptual system and the environment, rather than the subject, that produces the contents of the perception. So, taking the token-reflexive rule literally would mean supposing that these alleged uses of 'I' in the visual system refer not to the participant but to his visual system or his surroundings. I do not want to press these problems; perhaps sufficiently careful formulations would finesse them. I raise these points mainly to make it vivid just what view we are considering.

The real difficulty with this line of thought is that it implies that self-consciousness is inseparable from visual proprioception, but it seems absolutely clear that visual proprioception is possible for creatures that are not self-conscious and have no grasp of the first person. This is another point which makes our topic so hard: we have to acknowledge a certain distance between visual proprioception and use of the first person, a distance that makes it a substantial problem to see how they can ever be connected. Although vision provides a great deal of information about oneself, information whose most direct articulation uses the first person, this is not because the visual information itself already employs the first person. Rather, the egocentric frame used in vision employs monadic spatial notions, such as 'to the right', 'to the left', 'above', 'in front', and so on, rather than relational notions, such as 'to my right', above me', 'in front of me', and so on. The question, then, is how the use of the first person can ever make contact at all with this monadic information.

We can dramatize the problem by considering the case of someone who is skeptical about the use of vision to find out about his own location. This person, we may assume, has normal vision and has visual information given in terms of an egocentric frame of reference. But he refuses to use the first person to articulate the content of the visual information. He demands some justification for doing so and can find none. The question is whether we can find it for him. This person might, despite his skepticism, use vision as a guide for action, just as an unselfconscious animal or child might. He balks only at the use of the first person to articulate the content of his knowledge.

Notice also that this person need not question that the world really is the way that vision shows it to be. What he questions is only whether it shows anything about his own location in that world. He questions only whether he has the right to use the first person to state the content of this knowledge.

At the reflective level, this subject is in something like the position of someone watching a film. He may watch as the camera pans and swoops and tracks. He may take it for granted that what is being shown really is so: perhaps the film is a documentary. But it may not occur to him that the film is being shot so as to display the autobiography of a single person; indeed, a film ordinarily will not take this form, although it can. Despite this, he may indeed develop some sophistication in his judgements about the scenes being shown. He may build up a picture of the total space being displayed. And he may develop a critical grasp of the way in which that world works, of what is really happening, as opposed to being an illusion, of when a regularity he has taken for granted turns out to be mistaken. But none of this forces him, at any level, to use the first person in responding to the film. What is different between this subject and our skeptic is that our skeptic may use vision in guiding unreflective action, whereas this is not ordinarily the case for a film viewer. But merely pointing out to our subject that he uses vision as a guide to action can hardly force him to acknowledge the correctness of using the first person to articulate the knowledge provided by vision. In the first place, unself-conscious animals and children can certainly use vision as a guide to action without having any use of the first person at all. And anyhow, it is possible to use vision to guide action without accepting that vision is providing first-person information. Consider, for example, someone playing a video game, using hand controls to affect what happens on the screen. This person is using vision to act in a space that he is not himself in. The mere fact that perception of what is happening on the screen enables the subject to guide his actions does not of itself establish that the perceptions provide the subject with information about his own location or movements, for he may not even be in the space seen. And, our skeptic maintains, for all he knows, it may be so with him.

4.2   The Perceptual-Demonstrative Model

One response to this skeptic would be to say that there is a use of the first person that is more fundamental than the use on which its reference is fixed by the rule that any token of it refers to whoever produced it. On this more fundamental use, the reference of the first person is fixed instead by the causal links through which one has self-knowledge, similarly to the way in which the reference of a perceptual demonstrative like 'that tree' is fixed. On this view, only when we take into account this way of using the first person can we grasp the relation between the token-reflexive rule and conceptual role. We considered the perceptual-demonstrative model in the last chapter, but it is instructive to look at it again in this context. One motive for the view appears when we consider understanding first-person judgements made by other people. Suppose you hear someone say 'I am hurt'. You know that the term used is governed by the rule that any token of it refers to whoever produced it. But you will not know what to do with the judgement, you will not grasp its conceptual role, until you know who spoke. Consider now the case of one's own use of the first person. One can use the term in the knowledge that its use is subject to the token-reflexive rule. Is this enough for understanding the term? On the face of it, if we think about this case on the model of one's understanding of someone else's use of the first person, this cannot be enough for understanding the term, for one does not yet know who is using it. And without knowing who is using the term, one may be using the term to refer but nevertheless not understand the use.

A parallel may be helpful. Suppose that as you and I sit in a meeting, the treasurer says, 'The manciple is a crook', and you, having not quite heard, say to me, 'Who did he say was a crook?' and I reply, 'The manciple'. Here I have certainly referred to the manciple, but it may nevertheless be quite obscure to me who or what the manciple is. My use of the term to refer here evidently relies on its having an established reference in the language, which may be known to you though not to me. Someone who uses the first person without knowing who has produced the token is in a somewhat analogous position. This person relies on the way the term works as part of the common language to secure its reference, and at the same time lacks an understanding of that use of the term by the speaker. But suppose we now ask: what is this further knowledge that the speaker needs in order to understand his own use of the first person? It could happen that one is in a group of people all standing in front of a mirror, and when one says, 'It was I who forged the signature', one sees in the mirror that it was the person in the red jersey who spoke. This would be enough to understand an utterance of 'I' by someone else; it is hard to see why it should not also be enough for understanding a use of 'I' by oneself. But evidently, this is not how we ordinarily understand our own uses of the first person. If I say, 'I've had enough', I do not identify the speaker as, for example, the person in the red jersey. The point is that I know that it was I who spoke. The further knowledge that I need to understand my own use of the first person, over and above knowing that it is governed by the token-reflexive rule, is typically knowing that it was I who produced the first person token.

This is what makes it seem that there must be another dimension to our use of the first person, quite separate from anything characterized by the token-reflexive rule. For this use of 'I', which states one's knowledge of who is producing a particular token of 'I', does not seem to be one whose meaning could be characterized by the token-reflexive rule. If we supposed that its meaning were characterized by that rule, then we could ask, of one's use of 'I' to state one's knowledge of who produced the original token, whether one knows who produced that token, and if one does and one's knowledge has to be stated by a still further use of the first person, then we are embarked on a regress, and at no point do we have a description of one's knowledge of who produced the original token of 'I'. We do want to be able to use the first person to state one's knowledge of who produced the original token of 'I'. But this appeal to the first person seems to be useless if the only way we have of characterizing the meaning of the first person is by stating the token-reflexive rule. So there must be a way of characterizing the meaning of the first person otherwise than by using the token-reflexive rule. Some such argument as this can seem to establish that the meaning of the first person has to be described without using the token-reflexive rule. It seems to lie in the background in, for example, Frege's (1967) distinction between the 'I' of communication, which can be characterized with the token-reflexive rule, and the 'I' of soliloquy, which cannot.

In the case of someone else's use of 'I', what does understanding require, other than knowledge that the term used was the first person, subject to the token-reflexive rule? The obvious proposal is that it requires one to be able to identify the person, otherwise than through their production of the word. So, for example, it will be enough to understand a use of 'I' that one know that the person who spoke was the Minister for Transport. And even in the case in which one has no prior knowledge of the speaker, still, if one can perceive him, it will be enough to know that it was "that man" who spoke. Now the capacity to understand one's own uses of the first person, subject to the token-reflexive rule, does not seem to depend on knowing that one satisfies some description. Perhaps all the descriptions that one would be most inclined to cite as singling out what one's uses of 'I' refer to are descriptions one does not meet; perhaps it is only wishful thinking that one thinks one meets them. Yet the model of a perceptual demonstrative seems more appealing. There may be a kind of self demonstrative, so that understanding one's own use of 'I' is a matter of knowing that the token was produced by 'this person'. On this line of reasoning, if we assume, what we can hardly dispute, that there is a use of the term on which it is subject to the token-reflexive rule, the first person has two uses. For we have to acknowledge that the self demonstrative just mooted is to be precisely what 'I' expresses; that is, we have to hold in place the point that my knowledge of who produced a particular token of 'I' is often most directly expressed as knowledge that it was I who produced it. And so we now have to characterize the sense of 'I' when it is used in this way, as having something of the force of 'this person'.

Only with reluctance should we take this step, which can seem so easy and indeed inescapable, of supposing that there is a use of the first person on which its reference is fixed not by the token-reflexive rule but in some other way. Many of the most distinctive phenomena involving the first person are straightforwardly explained by its being governed by the rule. Once we leave the rule behind, problems swarm upon us. Most immediate and simple is the question of whether the alternative method of reference fixing, whatever it is, is guaranteed to yield the same results as the token-reflexive rule in what references it finds for particular uses of the first person. If there is this guaranteed coincidence, then it is not apparent what advantage there can be in shifting to the new method. If the coincidence is not guaranteed, then we have opened up the possibility of someone using the first person to refer to someone other than himself. But this would not be recognizable as a use of the ordinary first person.

What might this alternative method of reference fixing be? The obvious proposal, as I said, is that the myriad ways in which we have self-knowledge are to be thought of as standing to the first person in the same way as one's perceptual knowledge of a tree stands to the demonstrative 'that tree'. But then we run into immediate difficulty over point insisted on by Descartes: the impossibility of reference failure in the case of the first person. Anyone who uses the first person manages to refer using it. This is a straightforward consequence of its being governed by the token-reflexive rule. But when we leave this rule behind, the datum that reference failure is impossible is hard to understand. In the case of a perceptual demonstrative, reference can fail because there is, for example, no one tree at which one is looking; whether or not one realizes it, one is looking at trees whose branches have become entangled, and there is no saying which of them one is referring to. The parallel possibility for the first person is, How can one be sure that the myriad of ways in which one has self-knowledge all derive from a single thing? Perhaps they do not. Then, on this model, one's use of the first person will fail to refer. But this is impossible.

A perceptual demonstrative can also fail to refer because one is the victim of a hallucination: there just is nothing there of the sort there seems to be. If I seem to see a mighty oak, I cannot use the demonstrative 'that tree' and succeed in referring to an ordinary badger, even if there is a badger at that spot and it is somehow implicated in the production of my hallucination. With perception there is a line between distorted perception of a thing and a pure hallucination caused by the thing, a line crossed relatively rapidly. And a hallucination cannot ground the use of a demonstrative. In contrast, the most radical mistakes about oneself are possible, consistent with the continued use of the first person. I may think that I am made of glass, or that I am a steam locomotive, and my experience may really seem to confirm this but these hallucinations would not deprive me of my use of the first person. The token-reflexive rule explains this immediately.

Again, a perceptual demonstrative can fail of reference because there is simply not enough perceptual information available to ground it. If I can't see the tree at all, I cannot refer to it as 'that tree'. In contrast, to use an example of Anscombe's (1975), an amnesiac in a sensory deprivation tank may still be self-conscious and may still refer to himself as 'I', despite the minimal information available.

We should also consider the possibility of reference-splitting, as occurs with perceptual demonstratives. Consider the demonstrative 'that shark'. If I have unknowingly been simultaneously in sight of a pair of sharks, so that some of what I have seen has been the doing of one shark and some of what I have seen has been the work of the other, this affects the reference of my term 'that shark'. We have either a case of reference failure, in which there is no answer to the question of which shark I was talking about. Or some of my reports refer to one of the sharks, and some refer to the other. Contrast the case of 'I'. We can make some limited sense of the possibility that some of what I take to be self-knowledge may actually be the result of someone else's being that way. For example, it may be that when I feel off-balance, it is never I that am about to fall over but always you. My sense of balance might be responsive to your position rather than mine. Or more radically, maybe some of my memories are Q memories, in Shoemaker's sense: they reflect the life of someone other than me. In this case, there is never any effect on the reference of 'I'. It is not subject to failure of reference because of them. And my various reports of them always refer to the same person. There is never any question of taking some of my uses of 'I' to refer to one person and some to refer to another. The reason for the asymmetry is the quite unparalleled work done by the token-reflexive rule in the case of 'I'. This means that I do not use my self-knowledge to fix what I am talking about. Rather, uses of 'I' invariably refer to the person who produced them.

One reaction to this might be to suppose that reference, though not fixed by the token-reflexive rule, is fixed by the potential, not actual, self-knowledge the subject has, by what the subject would find out about himself were conditions better. But this appeal to counterfactuals seems unlikely to help. Consider once again the amnesiac in the sensory deprivation tank. Perhaps he is kept alive only by being in the tank, so if he were removed, he would not find out who he is but would simply expire. All that there is to his possession of "potential" here seems to be that he is the very person who is producing the tokens of 'I'. But then what we have here is just an appeal to the token-reflexive rule as fixing reference, and the talk about potential is a smoke screen.

Another reaction would be to suppose that these problems arise because we are thinking that knowledge of one's physical properties serves to fix reference, whereas we ought to be considering only knowledge of one's psychological properties. This proposal has to be distinguished from the view that treats the first person as being in some sense equivalent to a definite description 'the subject of these experiences'. As we have seen already, this view treats the self as a hypothesized bearer of psychological characteristics, which we directly encounter. It thus has some difficulty in explaining how one knows that all the experiences one directly encounters have but a single bearer. The view I want to consider now makes subtler use of our knowledge of our psychological states. It keeps the model of the first person as a perceptual demonstrative but proposes that knowledge of one's psychological states plays the same role, in self-reference, as does knowledge of perceived properties in the case of a perceptual demonstrative. To make the proposal fully explicit, we need a statement of the role that perceived properties do play in the case of a perceptual demonstrative. But I think we can resolve the issue without having to use any such explicit theory.

The most obvious problem is that I can have noninferential knowledge of the experiences of another person. Suppose, for example, that we are at a large dinner, watching some scene being enacted at the other end of the table. Suddenly, in a flash of insight, I think, 'He's jealous! How amazing!' There may be no inference here, just the flash of perception. If you ask me how I know about his jealousy, the answer may be, 'It went through him like a shock.' So when I watch the experiences of another person, I can noninferentially know his experiences. If this kind of link enables me to refer to myself, it ought also to enable me to refer to him. But then the present proposal has failed to articulate what is distinctive about first-person reference, about reference to myself. The obvious answer is that the inner demonstrative has to exploit my relation to experiences that are mine. But this is not enough. Suppose that I am watching a scene in a wall mirror and suddenly see a face twist with jealousy. On the present approach, I can construct a demonstrative referring to that person, using the link with his psychological states. And the person in question may be me. But I might not realize that it is me. Perhaps the face is so distorted by the pain of jealousy that I do not recognize it, and perhaps the jealousy is something I could not acknowledge as my own. What we have in this case is still not first-person reference, even though I am using an epistemic link I have to my own psychological states. What we need, evidently, is a characterization of the epistemic link that will allow me to use it only for first-person identification of the bearer of the psychological states. There is an obvious proposal here: the epistemic link we need is one on which the psychological states I encounter are given to me as my states. But then the use of the first person is already appearing in the account of the perceptual link, rather than being explained in terms of the link. The fact that the first person appears in the content of the information is doing all the work here, and we have not yet understood how it is functioning.

We can approach the same point from another direction. Suppose that we ask whether it really is possible to construct demonstratives referring to other people that rely only on one's knowledge of their psychological properties. This is harder than it can seem; it seems possible only because when we know of the psychological characteristics of other people we typically have knowledge of their physical characteristics too, certainly sufficiently to be able to identify them by ordinary perceptual demonstratives. But let us set aside this knowledge of physical characteristics and ask whether we could really use the knowledge of psychological characteristics alone as the foundation for a demonstrative referring to someone else. On the face of it, we could certainly construct a demonstrative meaning 'that (psychological) type'. But what is not apparent is that we could construct a demonstrative referring to a particular person, on the basis envisaged. Even if we hold a psychological criterion of personal identity, we still need to exploit reference to a particular spatiotemporal location to identify, among psychological states, the particular causal chains relevant to the thing we are individuating. And this takes us beyond the purely psychological.

In any case, there are many types of psychological self-ascription that do not seem to fit the perceptual-demonstrative model of psychological self-knowledge. Consider, for example, knowledge of one's own emotional states. Possession of this knowledge is a verbal skill; it is a matter of being able to articulate the content of one's states. Suppose, for example, that one returns from a committee meeting. Mooching about one's rooms, one may experience an odd sense of emptiness. At length one thinks, or says, "Actually, I am furious at what happened. I just had to work so hard at staying calm." But then one thinks, "It's not that I'm furious; I always could see the argument on the other side. But there was an unspoken motive I find rebarbative." But perhaps that does not exactly hit off one's mood either. And so, on it goes. Of course, we may actually not go on at this length about our own emotions, but we all know people who do. This kind of dialectical process does not leave one's mind unchanged: at the end of it one's state is, by being more articulate, both more complex and more transparent, both to oneself and to one's interlocutor, than it was at the outset. Nonetheless, one is not just in a new state, for the whole point of the articulation may have been to try to hit off exactly what state one was in earlier. Indeed, one can go through this process when trying to understand a state one was in some years earlier and succeed, even though the earlier state was itself confused and inarticulate. This is a kind of self-knowledge in which one's inchoate state is given firmer verbal shape. But it does not seem right to say that in this case the relation between the state and the information that one has about it is causal. This misses the point that the articulation of the emotion enters into the character of the state itself; the emotion and the articulation of it are not separate states, one causing the other. Rather, bringing one's verbal skill to bear changes the character of the emotion itself. It might be said that there is still a causal connection between the earlier inchoate state and the current articulated state, but the type of causal connection here is not specifically epistemic. It is the same kind of causal connection that would hold between the inchoate state one was in at one moment and that inchoate state at a later moment, and hence even if one had not articulated the state and so had no knowledge of it. When an emotional state is articulated, one's knowledge of the raw emotional state and the articulated emotional state are not separate states, one causing the other. All we have here is a single, open emotional state. And the articulation already involves the use of the first person. The model of perceptual knowledge of the physical properties of a thing, the model of the perceptual demonstrative, thus seems completely mistaken.

The most fundamental objection to this whole family of approaches to the first person was in any case already set out in the last chapter. The point is that we have to understand how we have the right to operate with the first person in inference in the way we do: trading on identity without there being any question of our having to guard against unnoticed substitutions. The model of the perceptual demonstrative, however we patch it up, makes this completely incomprehensible. As we saw, the explanation is that part of the notion of inference being used here is that there is just one person orchestrating the inference and this together with the fact that all uses of 'I' in the inference are governed by the token-reflexive rule, explains how the subject can trade on the identity of reference without having to earn the right to do so— no license is needed.

The appeal of the model of the perceptual demonstrative was that it promised a way of relating the token-reflexive rule for the first person to the conceptual role of the term. It took the model that seems correct for understanding someone else's use of the first person, where one must not only grasp that the term has been used governed by the token-reflexive rule but also know who spoke, in order to make the connection with conceptual role. The proposal, then, was that in one's own uses of the first person, the connection between the token-reflexive rule and conceptual role is made in a similar way. It is not enough merely to use the term subject to the token-reflexive rule. One must also know who used the term, and one must have in one's repertoire a "deeper" use of the first person as a quasi demonstrative to express this knowledge. Through this "deep" use of the first person the connection with conceptual role is made. What we have found is that there is no such deep use of the first person. Whenever one uses the term, however deep in soliloquy, it is always governed by the token-reflexive rule. So, unsurprisingly, we have to abandon the model of understanding someone else's utterance when we consider one's own use of the first person. What we have to understand now is how this result can be reconciled with the first person's having the conceptual role it does: its use to express self-consciousness.

I think we can take it as a datum that any term for which the rule of reference is that any token of it refers to whoever produced it is apt for the expression of self-consciousness. Elizabeth Anscombe (1975) provided an example that helps bring

and the consequences which we can draw from them, are the primitive norms. They do not depend on an ascription of reference to the term. Rather, the only force of an ascription of reference to the first person is as an upshot of the norms that do govern its use. This approach would mean that the various bases on which we make judgements using the first person can be characterized, and this is really all there is to be said. It may well be that there is some demand for harmony between the bases on which we make these judgements and the consequences that we draw from them, so dispute over the norms of use is possible. But such disputes can be pursued, the claim is, without appealing to the reference of the term. This kind of idealist response is a familiar move in discussions of how one or another sort of knowledge is possible. The upshot would be that the self, the referent of 'I', is some kind of construct, synthesized around uses of the first person made in accordance with our ordinary procedures (Nozick 1981).

But this extreme view does not seem to be correct, as we can see if we reflect on, for example, the multiplicity of bases on which we make first-person judgments. There are many different bases that we use. There is my knowledge of what I am doing or am about to do, and my memory of my past life. There are such elementary phenomena as my sense of balance, exercised when I think 'I am about to fall over'. Or again, I may think 'I am being jostled', 'I am cold and aching', 'My fingers are tingling', 'My hands are clasped behind my head'. The list could obviously be extended beyond my sense of balance, my sense of heat and cold, and my kinaesthetic information. There is, for example, my extensive knowledge of my own psychological states. All this belongs to the conceptual role of the first person. But it is not as if just any multiplicity of bases can all be bundled together as bases on which judgements can be made that all use the same singular term. For example, suppose a community that uses a term in every way like our own first person except that in finding out how tall they are, they measure not themselves but some designated other person, making remarks like 'How I have grown in these last few months!' when the designated person is a child. This is a crude example, but we have to criticize their practice, since we can find no coherent reference-rule that would validate it. That is, we can find no rule that assigns a reference to the term in such a way that all the methods that community members recognize as good ways of finding whether or not to accept sentences involving the term do turn out to be good ways of finding out whether those sentences are true. The best we can do is to reinterpret their remarks so that we now understand their remarks about "height" as remarks about the height of the designated person and we manage to validate the practice so understood. This procedure assumes that we have some conception of what objects there are in the world so that we do not simply have to take any and every assignment of conceptual role to a term to have some "object" magicked into existence as its referential underpinning. The picture here is one on which the norms of conceptual role and the norms of semantic value reciprocally regulate one another and can be justified or criticized by appeal to one another. The relation between the token-reflexive rule and the conceptual role of the first person is that the token-reflexive rule shows how we can assign a reference to the term so that the bases on which we make judgements involving the term and the consequences we draw from those judgements turn out to be broadly correct.

Having reached this point, we might well want to go back and review the way in which we think about the relation between the rule of reference for a perceptual demonstrative and its conceptual role. Do we really want to say that in this case the rule of reference can be taken as primitive and the conceptual role derived from it? On reflection, it seems that again the picture of the rule of reference and the conceptual role being in reciprocal regulation is more likely correct. We begin with the bases on which we make perceptual-demonstrative judgements and the consequences we draw from them. For example, we might characterize the ways in which we can keep track of an object over a period of time, or from sensory modality to sensory modality, in building up some conception of what it is like. The rule of reference that we need to underpin this characterization again appeals to a prior conception of what physical objects are like and allows us to say that an object may be the same object over time or seen through different sensory modalities. There is an underlying realism in the procedure here.

Can I be more explicit about the relation between conceptual role and the way in which the reference of a singular term is determined? There is a sense in which the bases on which a judgement is made must be *in concord* with whatever fixes reference:

Concord The bases on which judgements using a singular term are made must yield knowledge of the object assigned as reference.

If we are given the conceptual role of a term, the condition of concord puts a constraint on what we can regard as fixing its reference. If we are given the reference of a term, the condition of concord puts a constraint on what we can regard as its conceptual role. The crucial point about this epistemic condition is that it can be met without the reference-determining relation's being an epistemic relation. It can be met in the case of the first person even though its reference is fixed by the rule that any token of it refers to whoever produced it.

There is more to say about the relation between reference and conceptual role. There is a need for a certain richness in the conceptual role if we are to have a term referring to an object. Consider the possibility of subjectless reports, of the sort pointed out by Georg Lichtenberg, such as 'There is thinking.' There is no reference here. There is only the response to encountering the psychological state: the cry of greeting, 'Thinking!' This kind of subjectless report need not be confined to psychological states. One could also use it for laconic reports of physical condition, such as 'Drenched!' Someone speaking and thinking in this subjectless way might make reports that constitute knowledge of the properties reported. And this knowledge might all be knowledge of the very person speaking. But this would not yet be any use of a term according to the rule that any token of it refers to whoever produced it. We do not yet have a term referring to an object.

There is a contrast here between the first person and the cases of 'here' and 'now'. Consider a child who has been taught to say 'Rain!' in response to rain. Is its use of this term genuinely unstructured, or is it elliptical for 'Rain here!'? An utterance of the unstructured expression is correct just when an utterance of the structured expression is correct. So how are we to tell which the child is using? If the child grasps the structured thought, there must be structure in his grasp of it. He must be exercising a pair of conceptual abilities: the ability to think of rain and the ability to think of it as here. If the child has these separate abilities, it ought to be able to exercise them separately. So, in particular, it ought to be able to think about rain at other places: 'Rain over there', 'Rain in the valley', and so on. If it cannot do this, we should regard its utterances as unstructured. If it can, this shows a grasp of 'here'. We can make a parallel point about the use of the present tense, distinguishing between significantly tensed and more primitive, unstructured talk.

Can we use this model in the case of the first person? The idea is that what makes one's judgements of *F*-ness into the first-person judgements 'I am *F*', rather than unstructured Lichtenbergian reports of *F*-ness, is understanding the possibility of other people being *F*, so that one also understands 'She is *F*', 'Bill is *F*', and so on. There certainly must be this structure in one's understanding of first-person judgements, but it does not seem to be enough to explain the difference between them and unstructured formulations. The difference between 'here' and the present tense, on the one hand, and the first person, on the other, is that the first person is referring to an object. Simply finding the above structure in one's understanding is consistent with the following possibility: one's uses of '*x* is *F*' in connection with other people ascribe properties to objects, whereas one's use of the form, 'I am *F*' is actually equivalent to the unstructured '*F*-ness!'

For one to use a singular term to refer to an object, there must be a certain density and structure in the conceptual role one assigns to the term. Consider the case of an ordinary physical thing, such as a table or a tree. We understand that the condition of a thing at any one time causally depends on its condition at earlier times. One of the determinants of its properties at a given time is what properties it had earlier, and this is so no matter how much it has moved around. The notion of internal causal connectedness is presupposed in our grasp of the way in which objects interact. For if we are to have any appreciation at all of the effect that one object can have upon another, in a collision, for example, we have to understand that one central determinant of the way a thing is after the collision will be the way that the same thing was before the collision.

We have to understand the dependence of objects on their earlier selves, to grasp that their earlier selves are only partial determinants of the way they are now, and that external factors may have played a role. In describing our ordinary thought, then, we need a distinction between the causality that is, as it were, internal to an object, and has to do with its inherent tendency to keep its current properties or for them to change in regular ways, and the causality that has to do with the relations between objects and the ways in which they act upon each other (Shoemaker 1984a, Slote 1979).

There is another dimension to the ordinary notion of a physical object. This is its capacity to figure as a common cause of many disparate phenomena: one and the same thing can figure in many interactions, and correlations in the upshots of these interactions may demand explanation by its having been one and the same thing that was involved in all of them. This imposes further discipline on the notion of a physical thing, over and above the fact that its later stages are causally dependent upon its earlier stages. Without the point that one and the same thing can figure in many interactions, something might be internally causally connected and yet capable of only one type of interaction, such as being perceived. But this is not how we ordinarily conceive of physical things. I want to propose that to refer to a concrete thing with one's use of a singular term, one's use of the term must display a grasp of these two dimensions of causal structure. In effect, the upshot of this requirement is that to use a term as referring to a physical object, one must grasp, along with the term, a range of predicates that can be coupled with the term. And one's use of these predications must allow that the later condition of the object causally depends on its earlier condition and that the object can function as a common cause of many phenomena. A condition of richness in the causal structure of the reasoning one can engage in using a term, for one to use the term to refer to a concrete thing is the condition of causal structure:

Causal structure   To use a term to refer to a physical object, one's reasoning using the term must display a grasp of the two dimensions of the causal structure of the thing: as internally causally connected over time and as a common cause of many phenomena.

Obviously, this condition applies to terms for referring to physical objects rather than to names for abstract objects, such as the numbers. I want now to look at how it applies to the first person.

Many recent psychological discussions that consider how one has a conception of oneself give central role to the notion of a body schema, this being explained as, for example, "a superordinate representation at the interface between sensory and motor processes that both internally and externally specify a posture" (Bairstow 1986). But whether this is really enough for the individual to conceive of himself as an object depends very much on just what kind of work the body schema is supposed to do. Consider, for example, the classic "moving room" experiment, demonstrating that infants use visual proprioception to monitor bodily posture. The experimental space was a set of three walls and a ceiling, which could be moved over a stationary floor. Children who had recently learned to stand faced the interior end wall, and the unit moved slowly toward or away from the infant. The optic flow indicates to the child that it is moving. To compensate for this, the infant leaned in the appropriate direction, falling forward when the end wall was being moved away and backward when the end wall was moved toward it. One interpretation of this finding is in terms of the "postural schema" used in mapping vision to action. But this kind of use of the body schema is hardly enough to establish that the subject conceives of himself as a physical thing. Intuitively, one might think the point here is that information about the self that the subject is manipulating is too impoverished to sustain by itself the conception of the self as a physical object. But it seems to me that the point has to do not with impoverishment in the information but rather with the use being made of it.

We can get beyond this very simple use of the body schema by considering an experimental paradigm used by Andrew Meltzoff (1990a). He began by showing that infants have an ability to imitate faces at an amazingly early stage. They will imitate faces made at them by an adult. Presumably, this shows some knowledge of their facial configurations, and this is certainly of interest but is not enough for a sense of self. Meltzoff also uses another paradigm, however, one that exploits the traditional idea that social interaction is the source of self-consciousness, i.e., is the basis of a sense of self. One standard notion here is that self-consciousness requires the conception of others as a mirror for oneself, that one can find out about oneself by observing the ways in which others interact with one. Meltzoff's paradigm has a fourteen-month-old infant sitting at a table. Across the table from it are two experimenters, sitting side by side. The infant has a toy, as do the two experimenters. One toy each. One of the experimenters has the task of copying everything the infant does. "When the subject banged the toy three times, the experimenter banged his three times; when the subject moved the toy, the experimenter did likewise." The other experimenter acted as the control, merely sitting passively and holding his toy. Was the infant sensitive to the difference between the adult imitating it and the other one? The upshot of the experiment was that the infants looked significantly longer at the imitating adult than at the control, they directed more smiles toward the imitating adult than toward the control, and they directed more test behavior at the imitating adult than at the control. By 'test behavior' here I mean experimental behavior designed to test whether the adult is indeed imitating the infant, sudden or unexpected movements by the infant, for example. It might be objected that this experimental paradigm does not really test for whether the infant is sensitive to the fact that one of the adults is imitating it; the paradigm shows only that the infant is sensitive to the distinction between an active adult and a passive one. So Meltzoff set up a variation on the original paradigm. Two TV cameras were placed behind the subject and in view of the experimenters. One monitor gave a live display of the current actions of the subject. The other monitor showed the video record of another infant. Each experimenter imitated the actions of one of the infants seen on TV. So here we have two experimenters each actively imitating an infant. The only difference between them is that one is imitating the subject while the other is imitating some other infant. Still, the infants looked more often at the experimenter who was imitating them, smiled more often at this experimenter, and directed more test behavior at him.[1]

As Meltzoff proposes, this kind of performance by the infant may well involve the infant in the use of a body image which it uses to monitor its own actions and to compare them with the perceived actions of the experimenters. But this time the idea that the infant must therefore be thinking of itself as an object seems much more compelling. It is hard to resist the description of the infant as thinking 'That man is copying me', and so ascribing some grasp of the first person to the infant, even at this prelinguistic stage. But why should the use of the body image in Meltzoff's paradigm be thought to have any more bearing on self-consciousness than does the use of the body schema to control posture in the moving-room experiment? It certainly seems compelling that it does, but why? It seems to me that what is so compelling about it, in contrast to the use of the body schema to control posture, is that it shows some capacity to operate with a conception of oneself as a common cause. One is thinking of oneself as the common cause of the behavior of the imitating adult over a period of time. The body image enters because, through one's direct, nonobservational knowledge of one's own behavior, one has detailed knowledge of the common cause of all that other behaviour, and so one can experimentally manipulate that common cause, making sudden movements, for example, to see whether they are imitated.

I said that there are two dimensions to the causal structure of a physical thing: its functioning as a common cause and its internal causal connectedness over time. Can use of a body image put to work the conception of oneself as internally causally connected over time? I think it can, once we make the distinction between long-term and short-term body image (O'Shaughnessy 1980). 'Long-term' body image is a settled picture of one's own physical dimensions. So this image might be changed as a result of having a skin graft, losing a limb, or simply growing up. It describes how one is shaped and sized and hinged, what possibilities of movement are open to one. The short-term body image, in contrast, describes the way in which one's body happens to be configured here and now, the particular posture one is in. One's current short-term body image, together with the long-term body image, describe all the possibilities of movement open to one. So these representations might be held to provide one with a practical grasp of one's internal causal connectedness. These representations show how one's future posture causally depends on one's current posture. Of course, it is a further question how one might set up a paradigm to test for these representations (see Lackner 1988).

So far I have been describing a range of bases on which one might make first-person judgements, all involving the use of a body image. These bases give us a conceptual role that is "in concord" with the token-reflexive rule, in the sense I explained earlier. The judgements one makes using one's body image really do all give knowledge of the very thing that produces the judgements, using tokens of 'I'. And the first-person reasoning used can put to work the two dimensions of the causal structure of a thing, so that the causal-structure condition is met.

This description of conceptual role is not enough, however, to explain why the first person is governed by the rule that any token of it refers to whoever produced it. So far as that description of conceptual role goes, we could have here, rather, a demonstrative with something of the force of 'this body'. This would be a term that stands to the body image somewhat as a perceptual demonstrative like 'that tree' stands to the perception of the tree. The reference of 'I' would be fixed as the body of which one's body-image gives one information.

A full description of the conceptual role of the first person ought to explain what differentiates it from such a demonstrative. One line of thought on this begins by remarking that so far we have looked only at the bases on which first-person judgements are made. But a conceptual role includes the consequences of the judgements. So perhaps we ought to look, in particular, at the implications for action of first-person judgements (Perry 1979). Yet it seems unlikely that such implications will help us here. The body image itself must be supposed to have some immediate role in directing action. So a demonstrative based on it, 'this body', might be expected also to have immediate connections to action.

To understand what separates the conceptual role of the first person from the conceptual role of such a demonstrative, we have to give weight, I think, to the fact that the first person can be used in judgements about psychological states. Only when we do this can we understand the way in which the conceptual role of the first person relates to the fact that its reference is fixed by the token-reflexive rule. You might say that this will not help: the same problem will simply recur one level up, as we try to differentiate the first person from an internal "psychological demonstrative." But this problem does not arise. We can make sense of the demonstrative 'this body', based on the body image, but there is no simple demonstrative 'this mind' that could be grounded in introspection: introspection only reveals particular mental states. Alternatively, you might say that there is no reason why the demonstrative 'this body' should not itself be coupled with psychological predicates, so that we have judgements like 'This body is thinking.' I think that to respond to this point, we have to leave the body image behind altogether in our account of the conceptual role of the first person. That we have to do this anyway is made vivid by the case of a patient who has no proprioception, no ordinary body image, and consequently has the great difficulty of having to visually guide all the details of his action yet who nonetheless is clearly self-conscious (Cole 1991). I brought in the notion of one's body image because it seemed to be used to conform to the causal-structure condition in our thinking about ourselves. But it is a fundamental fact about first-person thinking that the causal-structure condition is met at the level of psychological predicates. Functionalism in the philosophy of mind and the standard problems of personal identity begin from this fact. I do not want to pursue these ramifications here. All I want to do for the moment is to characterize the fact more fully.

4.4 Psychological Structure

How might one put to work the idea of oneself as internally causally connected over time at the level of psychological properties? An understanding of the causal dependence of my later psychological states on my earlier psychological states shows up when I say, for example, that my grief has turned to anger. But the causal dependence need not involve a change of state: my later anger might causally depend on my having been angry earlier; I was angry all along.

What does it come to, though, that there is this causal dependence? Why not think simply in terms of a sequence of psychological states without assuming any causal relations between them? As a model, consider a spotlight shining through heated oil and projecting a pool of light on a wall so that the colors on the wall move and change. Or more simply, consider someone doing hand shadows. The later stages of the pattern on the wall follow the earlier stages, but they do not causally depend on them. So cannot one think of one's own mental states in this way, as being a shifting or stable kaleidoscope with no internal causal structure? What difference does it make if one doesn't? In the case of the pool of light, what makes it evident that we do not think of it as internally causally connected is our pattern of expectations as to what will happen if there is an interaction between the pool of light and something else. Suppose, for example, another pool of light, moving across the screen, crosses its path. This will change the character of the pool for a moment, but when the second spot moves on, the first pool will be exactly as it would have been anyhow. These temporary modifications to the pool of light do not affect how it will be later, and recognition of this circumstance constitutes our grasp of the fact that the pool is not internally causally connected over time (Salmon 1984).

If this line of thought is right, what constitutes grasp of the fact that one's later anger causally depends on one's earlier grief is an understanding of what the impact would have been of various interactions with one's surroundings. 'If only I had known!' one might say after the anger has led to catastrophe. 'If only he had told me, if only I had seen her, my grief would not have turned to anger.' Once one can think in this way, one is thinking of one's own psychological states as internally causally connected. Since we are forced here to think in terms of the lasting impact of interactions with the environment, it seems that an understanding of the relation between perception and memory will be central to a grasp of one's own internal causal connectedness. For if one has to think of the ways in which one can be enduringly affected at the psychological level by the things around one, the idea that what one remembers depends on what one perceived earlier is surely basic.

We saw that the conception of a thing as internally causally connected gives one dimension of its causal structure. The other dimension is the idea of the thing as a common cause of various phenomena. What we have just seen is that the conception of oneself as internally causally connected can be exercised with regard to one's psychological properties. Does anything parallel hold for the idea of oneself as a common cause?

Let us return to Andrew Meltzoff's paradigm (1990a). Meltzoff himself does not remark on the role of common-cause reasoning in his paradigm. If we ask how Meltzoff sees his data as bearing on our use of psychological predicates, the answer is this: He focuses on the role of imitation of facial expression in providing an understanding of other minds. His thesis is that there is an innate capacity to imitate expression. He further remarks that there is some evidence that asking people to assume an expression leads them to have the associated emotion: making oneself look happy will lead to one's actually being happier, making oneself look grief-stricken will have the effect that one feels sad, and so on. So the hypothesis is that when an infant sees someone with a particular expression, it uses its innate capacity to imitate the expression, which in turn leads to having the emotion in question, so the infant now knows what is going on in the other person.[2] Of course, this is not intended as a complete description of a mature understanding of other minds. Freud, for example, could presumably have remained relatively expressionless while achieving his insights. Even at the foundational level at which it operates, the model needs supplementation. There has to be some explanation of how one achieves a grasp of the causal roles of mental states; of how grief, for example, can interact with other mental states and with the circumstances to yield anger. And the model depends on, but does not explain, knowledge of one's own mental states.

Much of the thrust of Meltzoff's work has been to insist on the cross-modal character of knowledge of one's own behavior and that of others. He suggests that the infant represents its own expressions in just the same way in which it represents the expressions of others: it uses a cross-modal system of representation (Meltzoff 1990b). So the child has no problem about knowing how to match up its own expressions with those it wants to imitate; this is part of the reason why imitation is so primitive. It would be perfectly in keeping with this approach,

I think, to propose that a child may use a cross-modal system of representation to represent its own mental states and the states of others. One can see the pleasure in another's face, one can tell that one is happy oneself, and the pleasure may be represented in just the same way both times. This proposal, which, as I say, seems in tune with Meltzoff's own position, simply finesses the need for the kind of approach to other minds that he suggests.

When we looked at Meltzoff's paradigm earlier, discussing the role it gave to the body image, we gave no place to the infant's grasp of mental states: we considered only its conception of its own facial configurations as the common cause of a series of facial configurations by the imitating adult. But it is possible to view the paradigm as significant because it is the prototype of an understanding of the relation between one's own mental states and the mental states of another person. It can happen, for example, that the subject perceives the adult as experiencing pleasure over a period and finds a common cause for that pleasure in his own pleasure. So the common-cause reasoning used at the level of physical properties can be echoed at the level of psychological properties. Of course, we are considering only the very simplest type of common-cause reasoning when we look at imitation over a period. While someone else might take pleasure in my pleasure, they might also be depressed by it, bored by it, or, to look on the bright side, take steps to prolong it. And there may be no single response: one's mental state may be the cause of a whole complex of reactions. Nor is there any reason why one should be confined to the reactions of one other person, rather than a social group. I am not suggesting that there is much social sophistication in the infant. What I am proposing is that Meltzoff's paradigm matters because it is prototypical for an echoing, at the level of psychological properties, of the kind of common-cause reasoning that one engages in with physical objects. And this kind of common-cause reasoning is part of the foundation for the use of 'I' as a singular term. When we have this kind of reasoning as part of the conceptual role that one associates with the first person, we have moved away from thinking that can be expressed by Lichtenbergian formulations ('There is thinking').

When one thinks of one's psychological properties as common causes of psychological reactions by other people, one doesn't just think of one's own psychological states as producing other instantiations of psychological properties; one also thinks of the other psychological properties as the reactions of other people. So one is sensitive not just to the production of psychological reactions but also to the identities of the people in whom these reactions are being produced. For this reason, an understanding of 'I am F' depends on an understanding of 'He is F'.

This remark meshes with current work by Meltzoff in which the very same behavioral repertoire considered in the experiments described above turns out not only to be used in infant imitation, and recognition of imitation, but also to test the identity of the person who is interacting with the infant. Having faced for some time an adult making a particular type of face at it and then after a gap finding another human figure in the same place, the infant will first, no matter what particular expression the new adult has, make the same old faces. The hypothesis is irresistible that the infant is testing whether this is the same person as before (Meltzoff and Moore 1992). If this is correct, the prototypes of the conceptual skills I am describing do indeed develop together.

Why should we accept the causal-structure condition on conceptual role, anyhow? The reason is that by meeting this condition, we delineate in thought what we are thinking about. This is how we have any access to the identity conditions of the thing we are thinking about. In the case of the first person, though, we seem to meet the causal-structure condition twice over. As we saw, we meet it once in our thinking about our physical properties, and we meet it again in our thinking about our psychological properties. This is what makes personal identity problematic. Even though we accept identity as a causal notion, we do not know—we are not given in our understanding of the first person—any way of knowing at what level, the physical or the psychological, the causal questions relevant to identity are ultimately to be asked and answered. In this the first person is quite different from ordinary demonstratives referring to physical things.

To say that object identity is a causal notion is to say that the notion of an object and a grasp of its causal structure are at least co-ordinate. In dealing with questions about the identity of an object, we typically have to look at various causal relations, and intractable arguments about object identity are typically arguments about which causal relations are the ones that matter.

Conversely, questions about causal relations typically also make assumptions about object identities. The causal role of a property typically has to do with how it interacts with other properties of the object to affect the causal powers of the object. One cannot grasp the causal role of the property without knowing the identity conditions of the objects that have it. So insofar as questions about causal relations depend on grasp of the causal roles of properties, they also depend on object identity (Shoemaker 1984a).

Despite that, it has been held that there is an impersonal level of thought at which all the facts about persons, including oneself, can be expressed without any use of the first person or any other reference to persons. At this level of thought, we deal only with the causal relations to which personal identity is held to be reducible. And, on this view, it is at this level that we can best express the most basic and pervasive concerns of human life, such as one's overall network of plans and projects, even one's very concern to survive. This reductionist thesis runs counter to the whole thrust of this book, which is to display how fundamental the first person is to conceptual thought. So I had better look at the bases of reductionism.

5

The Reductionist View of the Self

5.1 What Reductionism Is

Rousseau (1987) said, "He who pretends to look on death without fear lies. All men are afraid of dying, this is the great law of sentient beings, without which the entire human species would soon be destroyed." But we are accustomed to oscillate on the topic of our own death. On the one hand, looked at from our immersion in our ordinary activities, death is something terrifying, something hard to think about with clarity. The problem is not the expectation of pain and suffering that may be associated with death; it seems to be even more fundamental than that. Death is the end of everything, and that is what is terrifying. On the other hand, if we look at the matter objectively, it is hard to see what is so very bad about death. One's plans and projects may be pursued by others, insofar as they are worth pursuing. Life for most people will go on just as before. And we are certainly considering a very small disturbance in the cosmos.[1]

It is sometimes said that the subjective view of death has its own inherent instability and that what we deeply care about in survival can be had even if we do not ourselves continue in existence. That is, even if we stick with the participant viewpoint, the perspective from our immersion in our ordinary activities, death as such holds no deep fear for us. This can be brought out, the claim is, by reflecting on the following type of case: Consider the way in which an amoeba divides by fission. It may be that after the fission, we cannot identify either of the amoebas that are around then with the original organism. For they may be qualitatively similar, and there may be no way in which we can justify supposing that one rather than the other is identical to the original. It may also be, though, that the two products of the fission are sufficiently causally related to the original organism, and sufficiently similar to it, that if only one branch had taken, so that one of the fission products never came into existence, we would have been happy to say that the original organism had survived. As a thought experiment, suppose that humans might divide like this; that is, they split spontaneously into two humans. We have no reason to justify supposing that one rather than another of the products is identical to the original. And we cannot suppose that they are both identical to the original, because there are two of them and there was only one original. So the original has ceased to exist. But look at this situation from the participant standpoint. Suppose that you are about to fission. The situation does not at all seem as bad as ordinary death. Of course, there may be practical problems, but the prospect of having to deal with them is not at all as bad as the subjective panic, the terror, that the thought of one's own death can induce. Nevertheless, someone who fissions ceases to exist. This implies that the subjective panic can be subverted from within, as it were: without moving to the standpoint of a transcendent objectivity, from which no one's survival matters any more than anyone else's survival, one can reach an accommodation with death.

I will ultimately try to show that this line of thinking is in fact not correct, that the attempt to subvert the subjective panic by appealing to fission cases does not work. But I want to begin by looking at Derek Parfit's attempt to set this argument on deeper foundations by formulating a view of the self, an account of what the self is, that would directly undermine the subjective panic occasioned by the thought of one's own death. This position asks what it is whose survival we are concerned about and, by giving a kind of "exploded view" of it, tries to convince us that what we subjectively care about is not an all-or-nothing matter, that we can, for example, make sense of the notion of degrees of survival. So even if one ceases to exist, the things one subjectively cared about may be largely attained.

This reductionist view of the self demands a noncircular definition of the identities of persons in terms of more fundamental relations holding between more basic entities than persons. In particular, the reductionist appeals to bodies, experiences causally dependent upon them, and causal relations between those experiences. The reductionist is explaining what a person is in these more fundamental terms.

This approach will give us a kind of exploded view of oneself, so that when one expresses panic at the thought of one's death, one is in a position, from the standpoint of immersion in one's own life, to reflect on just what it is whose survival concerns one. The crucial point about the exploded view of oneself is that it is in a sense impersonal. That is, one can describe all the components of the exploded view and the way in which they are all related without using terms that refer to persons or that presuppose that persons exist. In particular, one can think of oneself, in the exploded view, without having to use the first person at any point. One can identify all the particular experiences, and the ways in which they are all related to each other and to the body, without having to think of them as *"my* experiences." This means that one can reflect on the survival of this congeries of experiences and the physical body, and on just why it matters, at a level more fundamental than the level at which one uses the first person. Once we move to this deeper, impersonal level, the claim is, we can see that concern to survive is not properly expressed as the desire that *I* should continue to exist. The concern to survive would be better put as the desire that there should be further experiences suitably related to a particular set of current experiences and this body. But once we have attained the deeper level, it is apparent that the ordinary concern to survive tends to be put in overly dramatic terms. Even after my death there may be future experiences suitably related to current ones. The case of fission makes this vivid. In a case where I undergo fission, there is a plethora of experiences suitably related to present ones and this body, even though I have ceased to exist. So everything that I care about in survival is had here, even though I have ceased to exist. Notice that this view has fought off the terror of death without moving to a transcendent or objective standpoint from which no one's survival matters any more than anyone else's. We are still operating as subjective participants; it is still acknowledged that one attaches special weight to there being, in the future, experiences suitably related to one's current experiences.

The crucial move here is evidently in the claim that it is possible to move to a level of thought about oneself and one's future that is more fundamental than anything involving the use of the first person. Everything depends on the idea that we really can dig down to such a level.

I ought to remark on the reductionist's use of 'the body' as a primitive in his reduction. This means that we have to resist the plausible idea that the identity of a person just is the identity of a body, for then bodies are not more basic entities than persons. The simplest way for the reductionist to do this is to point to the possibility of bodily transfer: of a person occupying one body at one time and a different body at a later time.

There is constant pressure, though, for the reductionist to renege on this: to exploit the difficulty of supposing that bodily transfer can happen, so as to make the notion of a body do work in the reduction that it really can do only if bodies just are persons.

The reductionist has also to give an impersonal characterization of what Perry (1972) called the "unity relation" for persons: the relations between the various psychological states and the body of a single person. The aim is to give a description of various causal connections that at no point makes use of the notion of a person. Fission cases play a deep role in the argument here. They make it seem that it must be possible to give an impersonal description of the unity relation for persons. For each product of the fission seems to be psychologically connected to the original self in all the ways that matter for personal identity, but neither product is identical to the original. So it must be possible to describe the psychological connections between the fission products and the original self without presupposing sameness of person, and that will give us our impersonal characterization of the unity relation for persons. Using the description of these causal connections between things that are more basic than persons, we arrive at our exploded view of a person. We can use it to say what a person is; that is, we can use it to say when a particular collection of things constitutes a person. Or to put the point somewhat differently, we can say that we are defining the identity of a person in terms of more primitive relations between more primitive items. The idea then is that the exploded view will allow us to see exactly what it is whose survival we subjectively care about, and it will show us that what we deeply care about is not simply the survival of the whole aggregate. With the reductive analysis, we can engage in more exact and discriminating judgements as to what we care about.

I want first to focus on the idea that there is an impersonal level at which we can talk about experiences, a level deeper than the level at which we have the use of the first person or any talk of persons in general.

5.2 Ascribing Experiences

Ordinarily, I think of my experiences as mine. So how am I to achieve an impersonal way of thinking and talking about them? It is often supposed at this point that the reductionist must hold that experiences can in principle exist unowned, so that it is simply a contingency that all my experiences are in fact bound together as the experiences of a single individual. This view has it that experiences are concrete particulars that could perfectly well exist without the person who has them. But this view does not seem intelligible; we can make nothing of the idea of unowned experiences. So the reductionist has to do without it.[2]

The reductionist might acknowledge that once we move to a level of discourse at which we do have talk of persons, nothing can be made of the notion of an unowned experience. Yet he may still hold that there is a more primitive, subjectless use of psychological predicates. This is the kind of construction that Lichtenberg identifies as 'There is thinking' or 'There is pain'. Here there is no subject. Similarly, the use of 'it' is a grammatical dummy in the subjectless 'It is raining'. There is no subject to which the thinking or the pain is being ascribed in these formulations. But this is not to say that we can make sense of the possibility of thinking or pain without a person who is thinking or in pain. Rather, the subjectless formulation belongs to a level of language more primitive than any at which there is reference to persons. So at this primitive level we cannot so much as state the proposition that a particular experience is unowned. Similarly, suppose that a child is taught to say 'It is raining' as a substitute for its protests when rained upon or its cries when it sees rain. This child need not have the conception of a place at which it is raining; for instance, it might be unable to make anything of the notion of its raining somewhere else. So the talk of rain here is prior to talk of places. But this is not to say that we can make sense of the idea of there being rain without there being any particular place at which it is raining. Once we move to the level at which rain can be assigned to places, we can acknowledge that rain must always happen somewhere or other. So we can say that talk of rain is more basic than ascriptions of rain to places, without being committed to the possibility of locationless rain. Similarly, we can take the subjectless 'There is thinking' or 'There is pain' to be primitive and to involve no reference to persons while still holding that once we move to the level of discourse at which we do have talk of persons, nothing can be made of the notion of an unowned experience.

There is, though, a problem for this approach. Suppose that I am using these subjectless formulations to report psychological states. Of course, I cannot use them to say who is having a particular experience. Nonetheless, there is a question of whether I can use the subjectless formulations only to report what are in fact my own states or whether I can use them to report both my own states and the states of other people. On one reading, the proposal is that we will get a reductive base by using subjectless formulations to replace both first-person and third-person psychological predications. So when I say, 'There is pain', this may be reporting either my own experience or that of another, though the distinction between one person and another is something that I may be presumed to have no grasp of. Still, there are distinctions that I must be able to mark. I may want simultaneously to say 'There is pain' and 'There is no pain' without falling into contradiction. If I can use the subjectless construction to report what are in fact the states of different people, I need to be able to relativize it in some way or other. Moreover, I have to relativize in such a way that suitable pairs of psychological ascriptions are relativized to the *same* thing. This is particularly obvious if we consider ascriptions of emotion or temperament, which we characteristically make as part of a whole complex of ascriptions of psychological states. We have to relativize in such a way that the whole series of such ascriptions is relative to the same thing over a period of time. The same point holds when we consider the rationality constraints on ascriptions of belief and desire.

There is an obvious problem about this. On the face of it, we want the effect of psychological states' being relativized to persons, in that two correct reports of psychological states will be relativized to the same thing just if they are states of the same person. But, of course, the reductionist cannot use the notion of a person in giving the relativization. Parfit's solution is to relativize a report of a psychological state to what he calls a "life." A "life" is apparently a series of mental and physical events; he speaks of "the interrelations between all the mental and physical events that together constitute a person's life" (Parfit 1984, 226). But plainly, not just any series of mental and physical events can be taken to constitute a "life" if the coherence constraints on the ascription of psychological states are to be applied to the ascriptions made relative to a single life. We need some explanation of when a series of mental and physical events constitute one life. The explanation might be that a "life" is the totality of things that happen to a single person. But then, in relativizing ascriptions of mental states to lives of persons, we abandon reductionism. We manage only a superficial juggling with grammatical categories if we insist that mental states be given subjectless reports and relativized to lives of persons, rather than being predicated of persons directly. The reductionist holds, though, that an impersonal characterization can be given of the "unity relation" for the life of a person. So he may say that reports of mental states are understood only when they are grasped as being made relative to one or another life and that one has grasped this notion of a "life" only when one has grasped the unity relation for persons. This obviously abandons the idea that ascriptions of mental states are more primitive than talk of persons, for to grasp the ascriptions, one must grasp the unity relation for persons. What remains of the reductionism is only the demand for an impersonal characterization of the unity relation. The reductionist may protest that he does not accept that two correct reports of psychological states will be relativized to the same thing just if they are states of the same person. The relativization might rather be to bodies. We might take it, in effect, that the notion of a "life" that we need is the notion of the life of a body. This has some initial plausibility when we consider ascriptions of psychological predicates to others. But that initial plausibility owes everything to the plausibility of the idea that the boundaries of the body are just the boundaries of the person. If we suppose that bodily transfer is possible, then we have to acknowledge that the constraints of coherence on the ascription of psychological states may apply across bodies, so that relativization to a body does not give us what we need.

At this point I want to consider a motive for reductionism not mentioned by Parfit. This is the desire to view persons as a kind of animal, continuous with the rest of nature. One factor here is the desire to understand how psychological predicates can be applicable to both humans and animals that are not persons. Obviously, both persons and animals can suffer pain and anxiety, for instance, even if we find it difficult to know where the boundaries are between species capable of suffering and species not capable. It is because of this that animal experimentation is controversial (for the epistemology, see Dawkins 1990). This means that there is a question about whether such predicates as 'is in pain' are best understood as predicates specifically of persons or should not rather be thought of as predicates applying to animals, some of which are persons and some of which are not. That is, in grasping what it is for something to be in pain, we may not need to use the notion of a person at all, any more than we need to use the notion of wearing a hat. It is just that once we do grasp the predicate, we can see that some of the things to which it applies are persons, just as some of the things to which it applies wear hats. Of course, at this point we have abandoned the original motive for using subjectless predications. It was anyhow never easy to see why we should bother to introduce subjectless predications if we are then going to relativize the predications. The question for the reductionist was whether he believes it is possible for experiences to exist unowned. The response suggested by the use of subjectless predications was that there is a level of discourse about experiences at which the question of ownership or nonownership does not arise. But once we acknowledge a need for relativizing, the question can be put in terms of whether there are experiences that are not relativized to one or another thing. For the reductionist who accepts a need for relativizing, the appropriate reaction is not an appeal to subjectless formulations. The correct response is an appeal to the existence of experiences that are unowned by any person but are owned by the things to which the reductionist is making his relativization. And these may rather be animals that are not persons.

If we do take this approach, then the unity relation for persons will be defined over psychological states that both persons and animals can have. It would not, then, be defined over emotions such as pride or shame, which can be enjoyed only by creatures that are self-conscious, that are capable of first-person thought. This, though, would mean that we were defining an impoverished psychological life, since much of what we think of as characteristic of a human mental life is in the first person. In particular, we could not appeal to autobiographical memory as a psychological state over which the unity relation was defined. We could not do so for just the same reason that we could not ascribe shame or pride to an animal that was not a person. All these states are in the first person. For a creature to be in such a state demands that it can "consider itself as itself, the same thinking thing, in different times and places" (Locke 1975, II.27.ix).

Does this matter? Can we not explain what a person is by defining the unity relation only over states that both persons and animals that are not persons can have, states such as pain or perception? It might be said that the identity of a person is quite different from the identity of an animal, because the identity of a person is not the identity of a body, whereas the identity of an animal is just the identity of a body. But the reductionist may resist this. No doubt there are many species for which identity is sameness of body: this certainly seems to be the right criterion to apply to jellyfish, for example. But in the case of other animals, things are not so clear. Suppose, for instance, that Rover, the aged family dog, has failing kidneys and a transplant is arranged. The relief one might feel here is quite different from the reaction one would have to the news that Rover's brain is failing and a transplant has been arranged. The thought that it won't be Rover after the operation is hard to resist. But it will be the same body, only with an organ transplant. The point is easy to miss because we are very often not concerned at all with the identities of individual animals. If there is a principle here, it is that animals with centrally organized and relatively high-level cognitive faculties cannot be identified with their bodies, whereas simpler creatures can. This means that even animals that are not persons cannot be identified with their bodies, so the reductionist who is drawn by the idea of giving a common explanation of the identities of persons and animals is so far not compelled to give up his view.

To be a reductionist, though, it is not enough simply that one hold that persons are animals. One must also be willing to give a reductionist account of what it is to be an animal, a reductionist account of the unity relation that has to hold between a number of entities for them to constitute a single person. Otherwise, merely saying that persons are animals does nothing to show how they can be regarded as reducible to networks of constituent objects.

One way of being a reductionist, then, would be to hold that we can give an explanation of the unity relation for higher animals generally, making no use of the notion of a person and defined over constituents, such as bodies, and psychological states, such as suffering, that are not unique to persons. The appeal of this view is that it would do something to show how persons can be part of nature, though, of course, a number of problems would remain, such as the mind-body problem for animals. As I said, Parfit does not give this motivation for his view, but it does nonetheless seem to be a reason for supporting reductionism.

The general problem with the whole approach of supposing that the relativized formulations can give the reductionist his reductive base emerges when we reflect that for them to work in this way, it must be plausible that they do indeed constitute a primitive layer of language, a layer which is more fundamental than our ordinary ascriptions of psychological states to persons. For suppose we ask what the most fundamental types of pain ascription look like. Among the most primitive types we must include ascriptions of pain made otherwise than on the basis of observation, ascriptions that insofar as they can be said to have a basis at all, are made because one is in pain, rather than because one observes anyone's pain. In general, when one reports what are in fact one's own psychological states, one's judgements are not made on the basis of observation. Here we acknowledge the need for relativizing one's ascriptions of psychological states. And there is certainly a unity in all of one's judgements about what are in fact one's own mental states, judgements made otherwise than on the basis of observation. They must all be relativized to just the same thing. But this unity is secured by the fact that these judgements are, as we might say, implicitly in the first person. These judgements unite all the psychological states that one ascribes in this way as the states of a single person. The fact that the same body is involved is grasped only derivatively, through the realization that the person has not changed bodies. The unity of the states reported otherwise than on the basis of observation is a personal unity. This destroys the reductionist's hope of finding a way of ascribing psychological states that does not involve any appeal to the notion of a person and is more primitive than our ordinary ascriptions of psychological states. Ascriptions of animal pain are conceptually dependent upon ascriptions of pain to persons.

Here we can contrast ascriptions of pain made otherwise than on the basis of observation with ascriptions of physical condition made otherwise than on the basis of observation. For example, there is my knowledge of the position of my own limbs, as when I think, 'I am crosslegged' or 'My arms are behind my back'. Using my sense of balance, I may think, 'I am about to fall over'. Or again, I may think, 'I am being jostled', 'I am cold and wet', 'My back is stiff', 'Something is biting me', and so on. These ways of knowing one's own physical characteristics are all implicitly in the first person; the thing of which they are all properties is identified as a person, not, if there is a difference, as a body. This comes out in many ways. The various physical predications one makes in this way are all true of a single thing. It is not as if one has knowledge merely that somewhere or other something is looking out of the window. One knows that the very same thing that is looking out of the window has something sticking into its foot. If there is a difference between persons and bodies, then obviously these physical properties are united as properties of a single person, rather than as properties of a single body. The same point can be made for the ability to self-ascribe these properties over a period of time. If bodily transfer is possible, then the totality of physical predicates I know to apply and to have applied, in these special first-person ways, are predicates that I know to be true of a single person, rather than of a single body. Finally, these ways of knowing physical characteristics are integrated with one's knowledge of one's own psychological states. If I know, in this special way, that I am in front of a window and that I am thinking about Vienna, then I know, without any need for further premises and with only a single inferential step, that I am both in front of a window and thinking about Vienna. All this means that these ways of knowing about physical properties cannot be expressed at the level of the reductionist's reductive base, for there would then be an implicit reference to persons. But it does not show that the physical properties themselves cannot be mentioned at the level of the reductive base. For there surely is a primitive use of talk of these properties that does not depend on the ability to ascribe them otherwise than on the basis of observation. The case is quite different for psychological predicates. For all other uses of psychological predicates depend upon the most primitive level, where one can ascribe them otherwise than on the basis of observation. There is no such thing as a level at which one uses the concept of pain in such a primitive way that one cannot yet ascribe it to oneself simply on the strength of being in pain. There is no primitive level at which all one's ascriptions of pain depend only on observation.

The effect of this point is to put pressure on the reductionist's conception of one thing's being "more primitive" than another. What we have just seen is that all ascriptions of pain, even to animals that are not self-conscious, are conceptually dependent upon a level of thought at which there is reference to persons. If we want to say that such ascriptions of pain are nevertheless more basic than reference to persons, that they nevertheless are available at an "impersonal" level of description, then we had better be prepared to say what we mean by 'more basic'. For evidently this term cannot mean conceptually more basic. In fact, though, an alternative formulation is at this point not difficult to find. We can simply use a modal formulation: these states could exist even though there never were any persons. The existence of such states is independent of the existence of persons. The problem with this kind of formulation is that, as it is usually used, it implies the possibility of ownerless experiences. But here there is no commitment to ownerless experience. It is just that the experiences may not be owned by a person; they may rather be the experiences of some other kind of creature. Notice also that the modality here relates to types of experience, rather than particular tokens. The owner of an experience may be essential to it: if a pain is had by a particular person, it may be essential to this pain that it was had by this very person. Nevertheless, this *type* of psychological state could have existed even if there had never been any persons. In this way, talk of such states is available for the reductionist's reductive base.

The first problem with this approach is that it does not seem to give us the kind of reduction we were initially promised: a deep, impersonal level of thought at which we have abandoned the use of the first person. For in acknowledging that there is no level of thought about psychological states that is conceptually more primitive than the level at which we have the use of the first person, we acknowledge that the first person is always in play, and we always have to hand the materials to formulate concern for personal survival, which the reductionist sought to finesse. The kind of metaphysical reductionism now offered does not speak to our initial concerns.

Once we have reached this stage, moreover, it is apparent that the reductionist must be able to characterize the unity relation for persons without appealing to such first-person states as pride or shame or autobiographical memory. For it is not possible that there could be such states even though there had never been any persons. This belies the practice of reductionists. Parfit (1984, 204–209) evidently assumes that psychological connectedness will be defined over states like autobiographical memory, rather than being confined exclusively to states that could equally be had by creatures that are not persons, such as pain or suffering. And it is not credible that the unity relation for persons can be defined only over states that do not involve the first person. Even though we want to acknowledge the possibility of amnesia, so that autobiographical memory is not our only concern, still, in giving a psychological version of the unity relation, we do not want simply to set aside autobiographical memory.

These problems arose only because we were considering a reductionism that not only used subjectless formulations to characterize its reductive base but also held that these formulations could be used indifferently to report on one's own mental states and the mental states of other people. We have seen that it is not possible to sustain a position on which this use of the subjectless formulation is conceptually more basic than our ordinary talk of persons. The reductionist might instead propose, though, to use the subjectless formulation in such a way that it could not be used indifferently to report on one's own mental states and the states of other people. This would certainly be closer to the use advocated by Lichtenberg and Wittgenstein, who plainly had in mind a use of the form that could report only the mental states of at most one person (Wittgenstein 1975, sec. 58). The reductionist could hold that this use of these subjectless ascriptions of psychological states is genuinely more basic than their use at the level of talk of persons. This use of 'It hurts' or 'There is thinking' is one that can be used only to report what are in fact one's own mental states; it relates to a level of thought at which the conception of assigning mental states to persons, and in particular, of assigning mental states to other people, has simply not come into play. 'It hurts' is a cry with which one's own mental states are greeted.

On this interpretation, if a particular use of 'There is thinking' expresses a truth, then so too would a use by that speaker of 'I am thinking', and conversely. How are we to explain this logical link? We might take 'I am thinking' to be the basic form and say that 'There is thinking' is, as it were, a primitive sketch of it: it is implicitly egocentric and really only makes full sense when we grasp it as elliptical for 'I am thinking'. But, of course, on this understanding of it, the formulation 'There is thinking' is of no use to a reductionist: it already implicitly uses the language of persons; it makes sense only as a crude approximation toward 'I am thinking'.

The alternative gloss on 'There is thinking' is to suppose that it is the primitive form, fully comprehensible as it stands. The reductionist has to start from this solipsistic base, where he can only greet thoughts with a cry, to develop a conception of himself as the whole network of these thoughts, and then somehow to work his way out to the conception of himself as one among a possible plurality of subjects, all of whom can have these thoughts. This construction is what will ultimately explain the relation between 'There is thinking' and 'I am thinking'. The reductionist thus faces the problems that classically lead to solipsism: given that in the first instance, I understand psychological predicates in such a way that they cannot be applied to a plurality of subjects, how can I then find intelligible their application to other people? He also has the problem of understanding how there can be subjects other than himself. For in developing his conception of himself, the thinker has no need to appeal to the idea of a particular relation between thoughts: every single thought that he can greet with 'There is thinking' just is one of his, and there is no need for him to appeal to a particular type of relation that one thought must bear to certain of his other thoughts for it to be one of his. But then we have no grip on how the thinker might find it intelligible that there are other subjects, internally structured in just the same way as he is. We have the classical problems of solipsism. The classical response to solipsism is to say that its starting point is wrong, that we have to begin with the ascription of thoughts to a plurality of subjects. This response seems correct, but it is obviously inconsistent with reductionism.

5.3   Causal and Normative Relations

There are other aspects of the reductionist's position that are still of interest. In particular, we can ask whether he is right in thinking that he can give an impersonal description of the "unity relation": the relation that has to hold among a collection of experiences and a particular body for them to constitute a person. Another way I can put the point is to say that the reductionist may still be able to give an impersonal description of the relation that must hold among a particular set of experiences for them to constitute a single person, that is, he may be able to give an impersonal description of the way in which the constituents of the exploded view are to be assembled to give a person.[3] I want to connect this thesis with a point already made. We saw that there is one way in which the reductionist might try to sustain his view of experience. This would be to suppose that the kind of "reduction" he is providing is not one that gives a level of thought conceptually more fundamental than that at which the first person is used. It is rather a reduction that appeals only to psychological states that can be had by animals that are not persons, even if there never had been any persons, states such as perceptions and pains. As we saw, this does not seem to provide a perspective from which the concern to survive can be reformulated, because it is not a conceptual reduction, and the first person is still in play. But in any case, this move does not accord with the practice of reductionists. They accord a central place to such states as autobiographical memory and first-person plans and intentions in giving their exploded view. These states cannot be had by creatures that are not persons, because they require self-consciousness. I want to propose an explanation of why reductionists give central place to these first-person states.

Consider how the reductionist might go about giving an impersonal report of a first-person state, such as recalling that one heard the chimes at midnight. If we give the report in the form 'John is thinking: I heard the chimes at midnight', then we run into the obvious difficulty that the reference to John is precisely reference to a person, whereas we were trying to give an impersonal description of the state. But we can here use the subjectless formulations discussed earlier and instead say, 'It is thought: I heard the chimes at midnight'. Of course, here we really need some kind of relativization of the ascription, but, it may be held, the relativization need not be relativization to persons. It may, for example, be relativization to a particular body. There is also a slightly subtler kind of appeal to persons that the reductionist has to avoid. Suppose that the ascription we consider is not 'It is thought: I heard the chimes at midnight' but 'It is remembered: I heard the chimes at midnight'. Here we do not have a direct ascription of the thought to a person, but the notion of a person seems to be involved nevertheless. The notion of remembering used here seems to depend upon the notion of a person. For it is not really being remembered 'I heard the chimes at midnight' unless the person who is now thinking 'I heard the chimes at midnight' is the same person as heard the chimes at midnight. The obvious response to this is for the reductionist to refrain from using the notion of memory in giving the kinds of reports of psychological states that he wants to use in defining the unity relation for persons. But as we have seen, reductionists do not in fact want to abandon talk of autobiographical memory altogether in giving their analysis. The route taken by Parfit is to define a notion of quasi memory that does not depend upon the notion of a person. He writes, "An apparent memory is an accurate quasi-memory if (1) the apparent memory is of a certain past experience, (2) this experience occurred, and (3) the apparent memory is causally dependent, in the right kind of way, on this experience" (Parfit 1984, 226). It then has to be shown that the "right kind" of causal dependence can be characterized without any appeal to the notion of a person. In general, then, the thesis is that the unity relation is a distinctive causal relation that we can define over psychological states. Even if we acknowledge that this description will have to describe relations between first-person psychological states that are neither conceptually nor, in the sense given above, ontologically more basic than the notion of a person, still, the purely causal relations between those states may be describable without appealing to the notion of a person. We can do better than simply saying that the relations in question are the causal relations that characteristically hold between the states of single person. So the reductionist says.

There seems in fact to be no causal relation, or set of causal relations, that characteristically holds among the psychological states of a single person. No such explicit reductive description has ever been given. And when one considers the wide variety of pathological cases in which there is causal disintegration within a single person, it is hard to believe that an informative boundary line could be drawn, in reductive terms, between cases in which the causal breakdown means we no longer have a single person and cases in which there is still but one person.

The very notion of a causal connection between two mental states does not involve the notion of a person. There is, however, another kind of connection between psychological states that does involve the notion of a person. One reason why it can seem possible to give an impersonal description of the unity relation for persons is a failure to distinguish sufficiently between these two types of connection. Consider the 'I' thoughts of a single thinker. They are inferentially integrated, in the following sense: from any two premises, both stated using the first person, the thinker is entitled to draw inferences which trade on the identity of the thing referred to in the two premises. For example, from 'I am *F*' and 'I am *G*', the thinker is entitled to move directly to the conclusion 'I am both *F* and *G*'. There is no need for a further premise asserting the identity of the thing referred to by those two uses of 'I'. In contrast, if one thinker thinks 'I am *F*' and another thinks, 'I am *G*', there is no question of either being entitled to conclude that anyone is both *F* and *G*. So suppose that we consider two Lichtenbergian reports of thoughts: 'It is thought: I am *F*' and 'It is thought: I am *G*'. To know whether we can trade on identity in inferences involving these two thoughts, we have to know whether the same thing is being referred to. But to know this, we have to know whether the same person is thinking both thoughts. This point applies not only to inferences involving propositions entertained simultaneously by a thinker. It applies also to the logical relations between first-person propositions entertained by the same thinker at different times. For example, it applies to the relation between a first-person, present-tense judgement and the subsequent memory deriving from it and to the relation between a plan I form at one time and my later decision that I should then put the plan into action. If I think at one time 'I am *F*', I can judge at a later time 'I was *F*' without needing to use any premise asserting the identity of my earlier and later self. What we have here is a kind of temporally extended inference. It is, of course, necessary for the correctness of the transition that the two uses of 'I' be by the same person.

It might be said that this does show the need for some kind of relativization of Lichtenbergian reports of thoughts but that this need not be a relativization to persons. For example, it might be said that these two 'I' thoughts each have to be relativized to a body. And if they are relativized to the same body, then it is legitimate to trade on the identity in an inference involving them. But this response only even seems to work because it exploits uncertainties that most of us would feel when considering questions of personal identity. Perhaps the identity of a person is just the identity of a body. In this case, the relativization just mentioned will certainly work, but only because we are relativizing thoughts to persons, and reductionism is abandoned. Suppose, on the other hand, that the identity of a person is not the identity of a body, that a prince can wake up in the body of a cobbler. In this case, the relativization will not work. Two 'I' thoughts might depend on different bodies and yet be inferentially related, being thoughts had by the same person. Two 'I' thoughts had at different times might depend on the same body and yet not be inferentially related, because the body is at different times inhabited by different people. We will not be able to get the relativization right until we make it relativization precisely to a person. Notice, incidentally, that relativization to a person is enough. That is, if a single person grasps two 'I' thoughts, then they just are inferentially related; there is no further question about whether the thinker is using both 'I' thoughts to think of himself in the same way. This is what is correct about the thesis that 'I' lacks a Fregean sense.

The reductionist will deny that he is responsible for giving a relativization here, on the grounds that he has no need to characterize the inferential relations among first-person thoughts. The only connections among thoughts that concern him, he will say, are causal connections, in particular, relations of psychological continuity and connectedness (Parfit 1984, 204–209; compare 226).

If the account is purely causal, though, it is unlikely to work. A great deal of causal fragmentation is possible in the life of a person, consistently with there being a single person there. In contrast, the norms of inference serve precisely to draw together the unity of a person. The unity relation for persons has to be thought of as a normative relation. The problems that we encounter when we try to give a causal characterization of it are problems not of detail but of principle.

I focus on first-person thoughts because they evidently play a central role in the psychological connectedness distinctive of persons. I think it is possible to give a description of the connectedness in the psychological life of a creature that is not a person, in purely causal terms. One might appeal to the direct causal connections between the psychological state of the creature at one moment and its psychological state a moment later. And one might try to characterize more specialized causal relations between particular states and their effects. In giving a description of the connectedness of persons, however, we cannot rest with this kind of account. It is distinctive of persons that they are capable of first-person thinking and that their psychological lives are organized around first-person thinking; they are organized around autobiographical thought. A merely causal description of this type of connectedness faces serious difficulties.

The charge is that a causal description is guilty of confusing causal with normative relations. We can draw a parallel here between reductionism about the self and a functionalist view of propositional attitudes. It is sometimes objected to a functionalist theory of thoughts that it treats as causal relations between thoughts connections that are in fact irreducibly normative.[4] So, for example, consider the relation between the thought that p, the thought that q, and the thought that p and

q. This is not properly described as a propensity of the first two thoughts to produce the third. The correct way to describe the relation between them is to say that the first two entail the third, and this is what we need in giving an account of what individuates the thought that p and q, what makes it the thought that it is. If this parallel is correct, then we can say that what is central to the identity of a person is not the causal relation between the thought 'I am F' and the thought, 'I am G', namely that they have the propensity to produce the thought 'I am both F and G'. What is central to the identity of a person is rather the normative relation between the thoughts, that the first two entail the third; there is no need for any further premises. The same point can evidently be made about the first-person thoughts of a single thinker over a period of time. What is central to the identity of the person is not the causal relation between the thought 'I am F' and the later thought 'I was F'. What matters for identity is rather the normative relation between the two thoughts, that the correctness of the earlier one entails the correctness of the later one.

We can pursue the point by considering the classical cases of multiple personality. The fact that it is a single human being that is involved in such a case means that the various personalities cannot be entirely causally isolated from one another. If one personality damages the arm of the body, that will affect the activities of another personality, which has to operate with a damaged arm (so to speak). We can envisage a kind of limiting case in which the various personalities are, so far as is possible, causally isolated, but in practice, this limiting case is not encountered: typically one personality will have direct knowledge of the actions or thoughts of another. Yet the causal isolation may be sufficiently advanced, as in the case, reported by Prince (1905), of "Christine Beauchamp," that we want to say that there are different people inhabiting a single body. So we might say that "Sally" and "B_1," different personalities of Christine Beauchamp, are different people using the same body at different times. If we take this line, then when Sally says, 'I have been to Vienna', and B_1 says, 'I have never been to Vienna', the two uses of 'I' refer to different people, and both statements may be true.[5]

Even in this case, though, we may think that the causal disintegration cannot be so extreme as to warrant such a description. And certainly there are cases of less complete breakdowns of integration where we may wish to distinguish between personalities, because of the causal fragmentation, but resist saying that there are different people inhabiting the same body. But then, how are we to distinguish between the statements of one personality and the statements of another, given that we cannot ascribe them to different subjects? In this kind of case we can use an adverbial approach to the ascription of beliefs and statements. We have to form adverbs from 'Sally' and 'B_1', so suppose we use 'Sallywise' and 'B_1-ly'. Then we can say 'C.B. says$_\text{Sallywise}$ that she has been to Vienna' and 'C.B. says$_{B_1\text{-ly}}$ that she has never been to Vienna'. Both ascriptions might be true; that is, C.B. might have made just those statements in just the ways indicated. But C.B.'s two statements cannot both be true, for C.B. cannot have both been to Vienna and not visited it, and the truth of C.B.'s two statements depends just on whether C.B. was there.[6]

The point here is that there is still a normative connection between C.B.'s two statements—they are contradictory—even if there are no direct causal connections between them. The project of trying to define the kind of causal relations required for the normative connection to hold seems at least difficult and perhaps impossible. Perhaps whether the normative relation holds is something that depends, that supervenes on a causal relation; but this might be so without a reductive definition being possible.

It might be held that unless two propositional attitudes of a subject are directly causally related, there is no normative relation between them. For example, if two different personalities of the same thinker are causally highly insulated, so that when one personality thinks, 'I have never been to Vienna' and the other thinks, 'I have been to Vienna', the thinker cannot simultaneously apprehend the propositions and grasp their contradictory character, then perhaps the propositions are not normatively related. This position has little to recommend it. It is quite obvious that if the thinker could simultaneously grasp the two propositions, he would appreciate that they are contradictory, and the reason for this is that they are contradictory, that this normative relation does hold between them. To say this is to repeat the point I made above, that there is a way in which we do not need the notion of the Fregean sense of the first person. Given two uses of 'I', the question of whether they are inferentially related, in that their user can trade on the identity of reference in inferences involving them, depends only on whether it is the same person who produced both tokens of 'I'. There is no further question as to whether he was thinking of himself in the same way both times. He was thinking of himself in the first-person both times, and there is no finer discrimination to be made among the ways in which he might have been thinking of himself.

This point can be made vivid by considering self-deception. We may want to think of self-deception in terms of a main system of belief and a protective system, which are in some ways causally interactive but in other ways causally insulated from each other (Pears 1984). In doing so, we need not suppose a network of homunculi, so that the different systems are different subjects of thought. Rather, we might use an adverbial analysis, on which the distinction is between x's believing$_{\text{main-systemly}}$ that p and x's believing$_{\text{protective-systemly}}$ that not p. Of course, whether one uses such an adverbial analysis is independent of what view one takes of the rationality of self-deception. But the adverbial analysis allows us to say that the view that self-deception is motivated and to be understood in terms of the distinction between main system and protective system is not committed to viewing these systems as the subjects of propositional attitudes.

These propositional attitudes, believing$_{\text{main-systemly}}$ that p and believing$_{\text{protective-systemly}}$ that not p, despite their causal isolation, are obviously normatively connected. Indeed, the whole point of their causal insulation, in this model of self-deception, is that their normative connection must not be made vivid. So consider now the first-person attitudes believing$_{\text{main-systemly}}$ that one has not been to Vienna and believing$_{\text{protective-systemly}}$ that one has been to Vienna. The question of whether these attitudes are attitudes of the same person and the question whether they are normatively related as contradictories are one and the same. But it would plainly be wrong to conclude from this that we could give a reductive account of the unity relation by appealing to such normative connections. The normative connections are no more fundamental than the question of whether it is a single person that is involved. The only thing that might make this seem unproblematic would be a failure to distinguish between the normative relations, which are definitionally tied to personal identity, and the causal relations between propositional attitudes, which have no such definitional tie to personal identity and can be characterized without appeal to it.

Once we realize the tangle of causal relatedness and causal isolation that can hold between the various mental states of a single thinker, we might well question whether we can reasonably hope to give a definition of just what causal relations must hold between two mental states for them to be states of the same thinker. If there is a rule, perhaps it is simply: one animal, one person. In that case, the normative relation always holds between 'I' statements made by the same animal, whatever the degree of internal causal fragmentation. Being the same animal just is being the same person. We have thus abandoned the project of characterizing relations between mental states while appealing only to the identities of entities more fundamental than persons. For on this approach, being the same animal just is being the same person.

Alternatively, we might hold that different subjects of thought can inhabit the same animal, and that when this happens, we can always point to the specific causal breakdowns that make the diagnosis compelling, without acknowledging the possibility of giving a general formulation of necessary and sufficient conditions for causal integration in a single subject. Perhaps no such definition is possible. Perhaps we can only say that the various first-person thoughts are normatively related, in that inferences between them that trade on the identity of the subject are legitimate, without being able to give any necessary and sufficient conditions, in terms of the causal structure of the subject, that are required for these normative conditions to hold. If we have to appeal directly to these normative relations, though, then, as we have seen, being the same person is the only relativization that will secure such relations, and the reductionist cannot characterize the relations between mental states that are supposed to constitute identity, without making reference to persons.

This section began with the question of why reductionists, in giving a description of the unity relation for persons, make first-person psychological states central. As we saw, it would on the face of it be more consonant with the thrust of the reductionist view to confine attention to the states that persons have in common with other animals and to attempt to define the unity relation only over such states. On the face of it, certainly, animals that are not persons have less complexity in their psychological lives than do animals that are persons, so perhaps we can give a reductionist account of the unity relation for such simpler creatures. The insight that makes the reductionist depart from this model in the case of persons is the insight that the relations between first-person states constitute the identity of a person. The reductionist's mistake is to suppose that these relations can be characterized as merely causal. In fact, as we have seen, the relations that matter here are normative, inferential relations. And in describing why these norms of inference hold between first-person thoughts, we have no choice but to appeal to the notion of being the same person.

5.4   Fission and Death

Let me bring these points to bear on the role of fission cases in the argument over reductionism. One role they play is to make it seem unquestionable that the notions of psychological connectedness that we need in characterizing the unity relation for persons can be described in impersonal terms. For it seems that an original self is psychologically connected to each of its two successor selves in all the ways relevant to personal identity, yet it can hardly be identical to both of them. So we must be able to describe those psychological connections without appealing to the notion of personal identity. One reply to this line of thought is the *multiple-occupancy thesis:* that in a fission case, what transpires is that even before the fission there were two different people, qualitatively identical no doubt, in the same place at the same time, who merely went their separate ways after the fission. Here I want to note only that this is a way of resisting the reductionist's reading of fission. For on the multiple-occupancy thesis, the psychological connectedness between fission products and the original selves simply requires personal identity. The products are psychologically connected only to earlier stages of the very same person; 'fission product' and 'original self' are phase sortals.[7]

Suppose that, with the reductionist, we resist the multiple-occupancy thesis, so a case of fission is understood as involving three different people: the original self and the fission products. How are we to use fission, so interpreted, as a guide in providing an impersonal characterization of psychological connectedness? It might be thought that in fact we already have a high-level description of connectedness: the relation that holds between an original self and its fission products. But this is in fact not impersonal. For what is a fission case? It is precisely a case in which, had either fission product not existed, the original person would have persisted. So we need a direct characterization of connectedness if it is to be given an impersonal description.

Once we begin the task of giving such a direct description, it is not at all obvious that it can be done in impersonal terms. Any credible account will begin with a memory of one's own past. But will such memory really be distributed to the products of fission? Suppose that I remember taking the children to the zoo one Sunday. And then I fission. Can both products of the fission each have the memory they would express by saying, 'I took the children to the zoo one Sunday'? If both really do remember this, then both must have taken the children to the zoo that Sunday, but in fact there was only one person who took them then. The fact is that both fission products have false memories. Each seems to remember taking the children to the zoo that Sunday, but in fact neither did. If both understand the situation—that a fission has resulted in two duplicates of the original, so far as is possible consistently with there being fission—then both may conclude that x took the children to the zoo that Sunday. But neither would be right to suppose that this is something that he himself did. (We could resist this conclusion only by endorsing the multiple-occupancy thesis. For then both products really could claim to have taken the children to the zoo that Sunday. But endorsing the multiple-occupancy thesis makes the fission case useless for grounding an impersonal characterization of psychological connectedness.) It thus appears that fission products are not psychologically connected to their original selves in the way that people are usually psychologically connected to their earlier selves. For people usually remember what they earlier did and experienced. Fission products, however, cannot take their memories at face value but have to distance themselves from them. They have to regard their memories as relating not to what they themselves earlier did but to what someone else earlier did. Here we see very plainly what is wrong in the reductionist's use of causal rather than normative relations between first-person thoughts. The causal relation between the apparent memory of a fission product and the first-person thoughts of the original subject is similar to the causal relation between the memories of an ordinary person and his earlier thoughts and experiences. We can bring this out by remarking that if either side of the fission had not taken at the time of the split, then we would have but a single person with an ordinary set of memories. This does not, of course, do anything to show that we can give an explicit reductive account of the causal relation. And the crucial point remains: that despite this causal similarity, a fission product, on realizing the situation, has to distance himself from his apparent memories. They are not memories of things he himself has done.

One might reply that this failure of psychological connectedness between an original self and its fission products is relatively unimportant. It depends on an extrinsic fact: that there was a fission. Had it not been for the fission, either product would have been identical to the original, so the relevant relations of psychological connectedness would have held. But whether the relevant psychological relations hold between a given product and the original surely cannot depend on the extrinsic issue of whether the other product is around. This response, though, simply misses the importance of the first person as a determinant of whether the relevant psychological relations hold. The extrinsic fact controls whether the memories the later subject has of the earlier subject can really be taken by him to be memories of what he himself did. And nothing could be more crucial than this to whether the relevant psychological connectedness holds. It is not an unimportant feature of our memories that they are organized autobiographically as the memories of the thoughts and deeds of a single person, as the memories of "what I thought and did." Anything that disturbs this organization, extrinsic or not, disturbs psychological connectedness.

Here the reductionist may appeal to what matters in survival. The reductionist may question the importance of the autobiographical organization of our memories. The psychological connections that matter to us, he may say, are preserved through fission. So what we have to do is to characterize those connections that are preserved. This can be done in an impersonal way (since identity is not preserved through fission), and this will give us part, at any rate, of the unity relation for persons. If this line of thought is to work, the reductionist first has to convince us that the psychological connections that matter to us are indeed preserved through fission. The kind of case we need is one in which I am, for example, lying in a hospital bed wondering whether the fission has in fact succeeded. If it has, then I have a double on Mars, say, who will in the future be causally isolated from me, so that he and I can in no way affect each others lives. On the face of it, it is hard to see why this should matter to me. In fact, even if I can see this coming, it is hard to see why I should care about it. So the psychological relations we do care about are preserved through fission. The task, then, is to characterize them, which must be possible impersonally, since they are preserved when identity is not, and identity can then be characterized in terms of them plus, perhaps, a nonbranching condition. So the reductionist argues.

But are the psychological relations that matter really preserved through fission? It seems to me that in fact, fission is not a matter of indifference. Consider the following remarks by Nabokov in the Afterword to *Lolita:* "Every serious writer, I dare say, is aware of this or that published book of his as of a constant comforting presence. Its pilot light is steadily burning somewhere in the basement and a mere touch applied to one's private thermostat instantly results in a quiet little explosion of familiar warmth." If this is an accurate report of his condition, then he ought not to be indifferent to fission. For after fission, there would be no one who had the right to say, 'I wrote *Lolita*'. Of course, it would still be true that *Lolita* was written; but this is not the same thing at all.

On first encounter, it can seem that fission cases provide a way of pinpointing what we deeply care about in ordinary survival, and that they show that what we deeply care about does not require identity. This appearance is brought about entirely by a failure to spot the fact that fission would mean loss of the right to one's autobiographical memories, my memories of what I have seen and done. The accessibility of one's own autobiographical memories, from every part of one's life, increases steadily with age (Rubin, Wetzler, and Nebes 1986). And there is an obvious point to this. Autobiographical memories are not valued principally as guides to future action. They are valued for their own sake. The fact is that identity is central to what we care about in our lives: one thing I care about is simply what I have made of my life. Fission would force a reorganization of the picture I have of life so far, even if my principal achievements have been of an order quite different from writing *Lolita*; perhaps they were entirely domestic, along the lines of taking the children to the zoo one Sunday when I did not want to go. The basic point here does not have to do with achievement as such; it has to do with the way in which various incidents stack together to make a life. Fission would mean there could be no thinking of such things as things *I* had done; it would deprive me of one of the consolations of age. Perhaps it is wrong to look for this consolation; perhaps it is wrong to want a sense of the significance, of the pattern, in one's life. But this can hardly be shown by considering fission. Of course, there can be such a thing as seeing the pattern in someone else's life, in viewing their life as a sort of picaresque novel. But there is precisely the distance here that makes all the difference between it and a sense of what I have done with *my* life.

Points parallel to these could be made for intentions. I may intend to write a novel: I may feel that it will vindicate all the sacrifices I have made so far if I do so. I may plan to marry Jane: I may feel that it would make sense of everything. If I fission, the best I can hope for is that others will do these things. Doing them may make everything worthwhile for the others, which is all very well but it is not at all the same thing as everything being made worthwhile for me, which was the whole idea. The psychological connections that matter do not hold between me and my fission products. The reductionist might try to amend things here by introducing a notion of quasi-intention, which might link me to my fission products, but there simply is no coherent notion here that both describes our ordinary intentions and might operate as a link in fission cases. Parfit makes the attempt: "It may be a logical truth that we can intend to perform only our own actions. But we can use a new concept of *quasi-intention*. One person could quasi-intend to perform another person's actions. When this relation holds, it does not presuppose personal identity. The case of division shows what this involves. I could quasi-intend both that one resulting person roams the world, and that the other stays at home. What I quasi-intend will be done not by me, but by the two resulting people." (1984, 261). It is exceedingly difficult to grasp what Parfit has in mind here. The first person has a special link with motivation and action: it is because of this link my intention that I myself should do something is connected to my doing it in a way quite different from the way in which my intention that someone else should do something is related to his finally doing it. A quasi-intention cannot be an intention that one should oneself do something, because it can be acted upon after the division. But it is not simply an intention that someone else should do something either. That would obviously not yield any kind of psychological connectedness between the person who has the intention and the person who performs the action, and it is not what Parfit wants. He says, "Normally, if I intend that someone else should do something, I cannot get him to do it simply by forming this intention. But, if I am about to divide, it would be enough simply to form quasi-intentions. Both of the resulting people would inherit these quasi-intentions, and, unless they changed their minds, they would carry them out" (1984, 261). On one reading of this, a quasi-intention is simply a first-person intention, such as the intention that one should take the children to the zoo. After the division, both duplicates would apparently have that intention, as they both might apparently have the memory of having taken the children to the zoo already. But given that both products of the division understand the situation, they should be as distant from the intention as they are from the memory. It is no more an intention that *they* should do something than the memories are memories of what they did. So there still would not be the psychological continuity between an intention and its being acted on that there ordinarily is. In any case, this does not seem to be what Parfit wants. He wants it that the products of the division should be differentially affected by the original subject's quasi-intentions, that they of themselves should bring it about that Lefty should roam while Righty stays at home. If one were about to divide, it would be extremely useful to be able to do this, but the project in detail seems incoherent. If the intention is to have the required direct connection with action, it must be in the first person; but if it is to differentially affect Lefty and Righty, it must be an intention that *Lefty* do this and *Righty* do that; that is, it must be an intention that other people should do these things. But then it does not have the required direct connection with action: why should Lefty and Righty be particularly moved by what someone else wants them to do, even supposing that they recognize themselves as the Lefty and Righty mentioned in the contents of these intentions?

Let us review the position. The argument we have been considering runs as follows: All the psychological connections relevant to personal identity are preserved through fission. Since identity is not preserved through fission, the argument runs, it must be possible to describe these psychological connections without assuming sameness of person. That is, we can give an impersonal description of psychological connectedness. In reply to this, we have seen that the psychological connections we have to consider include the ability to keep one's autobiographical memories and that this ability is not preserved through fission. Further, it is evident that a description of what is required for keeping one's autobiographical memories will have to appeal to the notion of being the same person. As we have seen, parallel points can be made for intentions.

There is, however, another way in which the case of fission can be used. As we saw at the outset, one motive for reductionism is the desire to show how, from a subjective viewpoint, the concern to survive might be freed from a concern with identity, so that, for example, one's own death seems less terrifying a prospect. The strategy was to provide an exploded view of oneself, a reductive analysis, that would enable one to attain a more precise and discriminating analysis of what one valued in one's own survival. We have seen that fission cases give no reason to suppose that such a reductive analysis might be possible, and that the only way for a reductive account to succeed seems to be to define personal identity in terms of relations between states that both persons and animals that are not persons can be in. This is an approach that few reductionists have advocated. However, there is another way in which fission cases could be used. We have seen that through fission much would be lost of what a person values: autobiographical memory and the possibility of acting on one's own intentions. But we might use fission cases in another way. Rather than using the first person to articulate one's subjective view of the prospect of fission, we might introduce another term, 'I*', which articulates a subjective view from which fission really is a matter of indifference. Using 'I*', we might elaborate a subjective viewpoint from which the panic over one's own death vanishes. This would be in contrast to our actual subjective viewpoint, which is expressed by the ordinary first person. The possibility of introducing such a term does not constitute a way of defending reductionism, since, as things stand, persons do not actually use any such term and there is not much point in trying to give a reductive account of creatures quite different from us who use 'I*' rather than 'I' in expressing their points of view. The possibility of introducing such a term is of interest rather for the possibility it raises of adopting a quite different subjective attitude toward death. The proposal, then, is that we could elaborate this attitude toward death without going by way of reductionism.

We must not minimize the depth of the change being proposed here in replacing 'I' with 'I*'. I can immediately remark some difficulties that arise in explaining how 'I*' operates. Is it to be a referring term? If it is, how does it differ from 'I'? One strategy is to hold that 'I*' is a singular term but that though it refers, it does not refer to a person. Perhaps what it refers to is simply a path in a tree of fissionings and fusions. The problem with this strategy is to understand why it is not simply a notational variant on a view that equates persons with paths in trees of fissionings and fusions. After all, 'I*' is functioning in every other way like the first person. Of course, putting things in this way would involve commitment to the multiple-occupancy thesis. For two paths might coincide for a time. But this in itself would not explain why the strategy suggested is not one that simply uses the ordinary first person but understands the notion of a person in such a way that the multiple-occupancy thesis holds. In general, any view that holds that 'I*' is a term, referring to *F*s, that replaces our ordinary use of 'I', will be a notational variant on a view that retains our ordinary use of the first person but holds that persons are *F*s.

An alternative strategy is to hold that while the use of the first person is replaced by the use of 'I*', 'I*' is not itself a referring term. It simply "expresses" certain psychological relations. In this case, we envisage a scenario in which the creatures involved do not grasp the first person and they have no comparable way of referring to themselves. This means that we are dealing with creatures that are not self-conscious: they have no ability to refer to themselves, in the knowledge that that is what they are doing; they cannot consider themselves as themselves, at different times and places. This in turn means that we are dealing with creatures that are not persons. It certainly does seem possible to envisage such creatures, but it is not so easy to see how one might go about taking up their subjective stance oneself.

One might hold that the use of 'I*' is to be thought of as supplementing, rather than as replacing, our ordinary use of the first person. This would mesh with a response to fission that begins with the following observation. It can happen that the mere fact that someone else wants me to do something gives me a reason to do that thing. For example, if my father wants me to do something, there are background reasons for doing it. First, there is the mere fact of his closeness to me. This is a matter of his causal relation to me: that he is my father, after all. There may also be interests and values shared between us, so that if he has on reflection formed the view that I should do something, this already gives me some reason to think that I myself, on mature reflection, would also think that I should do it; perhaps I even think that he is a better judge than I am of how to serve those interests and values. These are independent factors. Even if his interests and values are different from mine, I may feel that the causal connection between him and me gives me some reason, however slight, to do the thing. Alternatively, a public figure whose views I trust, though he bears no such causal relation to me, might have some capacity to affect my plans simply by recommending a particular course of action to me. Now an earlier self is connected to its fission products in both of the ways just identified. So given that fission products can have knowledge of what the original self wanted them to do and that they have these kinds of connection to the original self, these wants of the original self should carry some weight in influencing the plans and actions of the fission products. The use of 'I*' would merely express this special relationship between the original self and the products. In this kind of case, the use of the first person remains the basic, uneliminated connection between plans and action. If I am a fission product, I may well have a number of intentions that I* should do something, but this only shows me that someone close to me would like me to do those things. They have no bearing on what I actually do until I decide that I will act on them. As I have said, I do have some reason to form the intention that I will act on them, but this is not the same thing as having the intention.

The point remains that it is the link between what I plan to do and what I actually do that gives us the psychological connectedness characteristic of personal identity. Similarly, the role of the first person in autobiographical memory remains fundamental: it is what connects earlier and later judgements by the same person. Indeed, we can go further than saying that the use of 'I' has in fact not been eliminated by this proposal. The use of 'I' cannot be eliminated without making it quite unintelligible why the kinds of connectedness described above should matter. The reason why my father's wishes matter to me is precisely his connection to me; the reason why I might be guided by a public figure is precisely the relation between his interests and values and mine. Just so, the only reason why the intentions of my earlier self should matter to me as a fission product is the causal connection and similarities of that earlier self to me. The use of the first person is needed to explain why these psychological relations matter; abandon the use of the first person, and there would be no reason at all why the plans and ambitions of the earlier self should matter to the fission product.

In elaborating an alternative to our ordinary subjective viewpoint, then, we do better to consider uses of 'I*' that replace our ordinary use of the first person. But how are we to explain the term thus introduced? One way would be to say that 'I*' is subject to the following rule: each token of 'I*' may refer to the person who produced it or to any person psychologically connected to the producer. The term could function as a restricted demonstrative, like 'that tree', which can apply to any one of a particular range of individuals.[8] So there is the substantive question of how the term can be used to refer to the person who produced it. This is the price we pay for distancing ourselves from the ordinary first person, which is simply governed by the rule that any token of it refers to the person who produced it. Once we start considering a term not governed by this rule, there is the question of how its reference can be directed to the person who produced it. But perhaps the correct picture is that on some occasions of its use, 'I*' is subject to the rule for 'I', whereas on other occasions of its use it operates in a different way.

There is also the question how psychological predicates are to be introduced and explained if we do not have the ordinary first person. One answer would be that they are introduced and explained as predicates of persons, using ordinary proper names. This, however, means that we have to consider a language that has no place for the psychological statements made otherwise than on the basis of observation; it will have no counterpart to our ordinary use of 'I am in pain', for example, a statement that does not require the identification of an individual but is made simply on the strength of the fact that one is in pain. In this language, all psychological statements will involve the use of proper names, and so require the identification of an individual. It might be held that we can use 'I*' to plug this gap. We have only to consider the way in which it is used when it identifies the person who produced it, and this use of 'I*' will enable us to make statements such as 'I* am in pain' otherwise than on the basis of observation. The problem now is that this use of 'I*' seems to be exactly synonymous with the ordinary first person. And as before, given the centrality of the first person in our psychological lives, it will seem that all other uses of 'I*' have their motivational force because of their connection with this fundamental use of 'I*', on which it is a version of the first person. There will have been no deep conceptual change. If we want to elaborate a genuinely subjective view on which identity does not matter in survival, we will need a deeply articulated account of 'I*' and its role in explaining psychological predicates. Until we have such an account, of course, there is always the response from the standpoint of a transcendent objectivity: that no one matters any more than anyone else and that identity does not matter because survival does not matter.

This connects with the final remark I wish to make, on the bearing of these points on reductionism. I have stressed the central place of the first person. And at some points the reductionist will no doubt want to protest that what I have done or plan to do is of no cosmic significance and that there is something almost unbearably egocentric about assigning the first person the central place I have given it. Though I have some sympathy with this protest, it reflects a poor grasp of the place that I have assigned to the first person, and it gives no comfort to the reductionist. I have been trying to establish the character of the psychological connectedness that typifies persons, and it is here that I have said we must give central place to the first person. It is, of course, quite right to say that we often give ourselves more weight than we ought to in our deliberations, and perhaps we always give ourselves more weight than we ought to. This point is indifferent to the specific account we give of the notion of a person and the psychological connectedness characteristic of persons: the point could be made whether or not reductionism about persons is true. My present concern is not with this issue. I have been trying to do something rather different: to explore the question whether the fission cases give any reason to suppose that psychological connectedness can be described in impersonal terms. We have been considering a line of thought that says that the psychological connections that subjectively matter in survival are all preserved through fission, even though personal identity is not, so that it must be possible to describe those connections impersonally. I have been pointing out that the psychological connections that matter in survival have an ineliminably first-person character and consequently cannot be preserved through fission. It is quite consistent with this to hold that in the end, survival does not matter at all, from the standpoint of the cosmos. Survival is one thing, the cosmos another.

6

Conceptual Structure and Self-Consciousness

6.1   A Repertoire of Concepts

Someone who can think is a possessor of concepts. That is, he or she has a network of conceptual abilities, used over and over again, each one coupled with others in inexhaustibly many different combinations. The point is reflected in the use that we make of the idea of someone's vocabulary. There is a causal structure in competence with language: we understand a sentence by bringing to bear a network of competences with various words, and these competences can be recombined with each other in endlessly many ways. So the extent of someone's competence with a language is not best indicated by reeling off all the sentences he knows. The best approach is to list the words he knows, which is why we have a use for the notion of someone's vocabulary. I am interested in language only because I am interested in thought, though, and the relation between language and thought is not entirely straightforward. So I will speak not of a vocabulary but of a repertoire of concepts. To have a repertoire of concepts is to have a certain causal structure in one's thinking. One uses a cluster of conceptual abilities that one stably possesses over quite a long period, perhaps the good majority of one's life.

This stability in conceptual abilities is fundamental to our cognitive lives. The uses that we make of memory and perception depend on it. As one travels through life, one sees and does various things, and uses one's conceptual abilities at the time in making up one's mind about what is going on. If one is to use a past assessment of the situation years later in remembering what happened, the conceptual abilities that one exercises years later must be the very same abilities that one had earlier. If one simply had different clusters of conceptual abilities at various times, then one would lose contact with one's past self; one could have no communication from it. And, of course, in memory one uses the assessments that one made of many situations, perhaps separated by considerable periods of time, as they were happening. So again, all these assessments must use the same stable set of conceptual abilities. And finally, it is very rare that someone starts from scratch in constructing a narrative of his past life. Usually one relies and elaborates on a narrative constructed earlier, which itself relies on still earlier narratives, and so on back to the social constructions of episodic memory in early childhood. It is obviously vital that one has the same stable complex of conceptual abilities to draw on throughout.

Of course, one's repertoire of concepts expands over time, and one's ability to apply the concepts one has becomes more sophisticated. This is perhaps most striking in the case of psychological concepts. One thinks back and says, 'I see now that she was passionate about him', or 'He was angry with me, though I didn't realize it then', as one reflects on childhood experiences. One did not have those concepts then, or if one did, one could not apply them sure-footedly. But this kind of thing is possible only against a background of possessing, then and now, a solid, stable core of conceptual abilities that one uses then and now to characterize the basics of the situation and its role in one's life and in local history. Shrinkage in one's repertoire of concepts is also possible. This is most familiar in the case of relatively technical terms, as when one struggles to think what a monomer is and whether it is different from a metamer, things one used to know.

I can be more explicit about just how the stability in one's conceptual abilities is put to work. It is not just that back then one made a number of judgements about the state of play, so that one now needs to have retained one's conceptual skills if one is to have any access at all to what one thought then. In constructing a narrative of one's past life, one does not simply juxtapose a number of judgements made at different times; one must be able to recognize the inferential relations between these judgements. If one is putting together the story of one's encounters with Bill over the years, for example, one has to be able to trade on the identity of the person whom all these judgements concern, in reasoning it through. And what gives one the right to do so is not some laborious proof one devises but the brute fact that in all these judgements one is exercising a single conceptual ability, the capacity to think about him. The brute fact that a single conceptual ability is in play in one's grasp of various judgements about Bill is what gives one the right to regard them all as inferentially connected.

So far in this book I have been describing the basic conceptual skills implicated in the idea of oneself as causally structured in two dimensions: as internally causally connected over time, in that one's later states causally depend, in part, on one's earlier states, and as a common cause of various correlated effects in the world around one. Because this understanding of self is so fundamental to, and pervasive in, ordinary human life, the conceptual skills implicated in it are bound to be part of the stable core of conceptual skills that one has through one's life.

Let me review what these conceptual skills are. Let us begin with the idea of oneself as internally causally connected over time. Or better, let us begin merely with what is required for the idea of particular past times, describe the conceptual skills involved, and then come back to look at their relation to the idea of oneself as internally causally connected.

We saw in chapter 2 that to identify particular past times, one uses the capacity to identify persisting physical objects. It is by thinking about particular persisting objects and the causal relations within and among them that one can differentiate, by understanding the causal relations between, different times that occur at the same phase of a cycle. So one uses the capacity to identify physical things. And this general capacity is exercised in a range of particular singular modes of thought. Correlatively, one uses conceptions of the physical properties of things in articulating the causal relations within and between them. One uses one's grasp of what I earlier called an explicit physics, involving generalizations about the ways in which objects behave. One has the general capacity to think about shape properties, for example, which is exercised in a multitude of conceptions of particular shapes. And the generalizations of one's explicit physics may be pitched at varying levels of abstraction: as relating to all shapes, as in 'things of the same shape and size will fit in the same boxes', as relating to particular types of shape, such as 'pointed', or as relating to specific shapes, such as 'spherical'. So one has a range of singular modes of thought about particular objects and a host of conceptions of physical properties. And one has also the explicit physics of our environment. Now one has these conceptual skills over a period of time and repeatedly brings them to bear on the objects one encounters. For the basic physics to have this dynamic character, one must be able to combine and recombine the singular modes of thought with one's conceptions of the properties: one must be able to think of any of the objects as having any of the properties.

This temporal framework is put to work in thinking about one's own past interactions with the things around one. Of course, one can think of oneself as merely one among many physical objects—at the level of one's physical properties only. But as I remarked earlier, self-consciousness requires that one think of one's psychological states as produced by the things around one and as themselves affecting one's surroundings. Centrally, we think of our perceptions as causally dependent on the way things are around us: what one sees depends on what is there to be seen. And perception leaves traces: what one remembers depends in part on what one perceives.

Grasp of spatial relations is central in all these types of thinking. Again, one has a general capacity to think reflectively—at a level where causal significance is not exhausted by implications for action—about directions, speeds, and distances, a capacity exercised in having the conception of particular directions, speeds, and distances of the things one encounters. This has a fundamental role in our explicit physics, because we think of spatial contact as the condition of causal interaction (Spelke 1988). And spatial thinking plays a similar role in understanding our perceptual interactions with the world. In the case of touch, the condition is again spatial contact: to touch the thing you must touch it. But in general the condition of causal interaction in perception is not contact. The analogue of 'no action at a distance' is provided by our grasp of the enabling conditions of perception. For example, to see something one must be appropriately located with respect to it, one must look in the right direction, and there must be nothing in the way. So in both the physical and the psychological cases, one's understanding of the conditions of causal interaction is provided by one's reflective understanding of spatial relations.

Let us now review how this repertoire of concepts relates to the conception of oneself as internally causally connected over time. We do not think of ourselves as being merely in a sequence of states; we have the idea that our earlier states causally affect our later condition. In this we can contrast the way one thinks of oneself with the way one thinks of, for example, the pool of light thrown by a street lamp. The pool of light has a sequence of states: it has various shadows thrown across it as people pass by, for example. But it is not internally causally connected. What does this difference come to? It is not just that the later states of something internally causally connected are counterfactually dependent on the earlier states; it might be true of the pool of light that it would not now be shadowed in one way if it had not earlier been shadowed in another way. To get at the difference between the way in which we think of ourselves as internally causally connected and the way in which we think of the pool of light, we have to consider the differences between them as they relate to their interactions with other objects. The point is that we can be marked by our interactions with other things, whereas the pool of light has no impression made on it by the shadows cast on it, they leave no mark (Salmon 1984). So our understanding of memory as the mark left on one by past perceptual interactions is crucial here. And this understanding exploits all of the conceptual repertoire described so far.

What about the conception of oneself as a common cause of various correlated effects in the world around one? As we saw, this can be exercised in either a physical or a psychological mode of thought, and it is the psychological mode that matters for self-consciousness. What is required is that one should have a range of capacities to think about psychological states and the ability to think of one's own psychological states as the causes of the mental states of other people. So as one of the bases of grasp of the first person, one needs an ability to identify other people and a capacity to ascribe psychological properties both to oneself and to others. Such is the repertoire of concepts implicated in an understanding of the two dimensions of one's causal structure, which we saw to be the foundation of grasp of the first person.

Possession of this repertoire of conceptual abilities is what constitutes possession of concepts. Possessing this stable core of conceptual skills through one's life marks the difference between someone capable of conceptual thought and an animal with some other, perhaps more primitive, type of representational system. Of course, any representation system is structured: anything recognizable as a representational system at all will involve the possibility of operations being performed by the subject on its representations, and this will require there to be structure in the representations to be exploited in these operations. What is distinctive of human conceptual thinking is that it has the structure just described.

6.2 Truth, Structure, and the Simple Theory

Philosophers sometimes dispute over whether structure in a thought requires there to be structure in grasp of the thought. I want now to consider the way in which our grasp of thoughts exploits the fact that we have the conceptual repertoire just described. Someone who has these skills may be said to grasp a simple theory of perception and action. I do not mean that he grasps a schematic theory, stated using abstract concepts. Most people do not have an explicit grasp of the very abstract ideas required in a fully general statement of the theory. What I mean by 'grasp of a simple theory of perception and action' is better described as a skill: the ability to generate causal explanations of particular perceptions or the consequences of particular actions. The actual explanations are all at the level of the concrete particular. By grasp of the "theory" I mean simply the ability to give such particular explanations. The ability to give such explanations could be, but evidently need not be, underwritten by an explicit grasp of a fully general schematic theory. Grasp of the simple theory, in this sense, is just a part of having the conceptual repertoire already described.

Grasp of the simple theory is fundamental to our understanding of what it is for ordinary empirical statements to be true or false and the way in which this understanding relates to our ability to use various different methods to establish or refute the statements. Suppose, for example, that I suddenly realize that I am without my umbrella, though I certainly had it when I left the Tourist Bureau. I think the thing through and realize I must have left it in the bank. So now I know where it is. Now there are two features of this example to which I would like to draw your attention. First, it is not particularly plausible to suppose that it is part of the way in which one would explain the meaning of 'My umbrella is in the bank' that one point out the possibility of establishing its truth by this kind of reasoning. The reasoning may principally turn on reconstruction of my route from the Tourist Bureau and the elimination of alternatives; it may be highly specific to the context. Second, it cannot be that only through the chain of reasoning can the whereabouts of my umbrella be established. That is, if my reasoning is right, it must also be possible to establish by observation that the umbrella is in the bank. Something has gone wrong if one holds a view on which it would be coherent to suppose that my umbrella is in the bank, all right, but it is impossible to establish this by observation, that the only way in which this can be discovered is by the reasoning about where I must have left it.

How are we to explain these two features of our use of the statement? One approach is suggested by a verificationist model of our understanding of mathematical statements that distinguishes between canonical and noncanonical methods of proof. On this model, we explain the meaning of a mathematical statement by laying down what is to count as a canonical proof of it. If we ask how there can be such a thing as noncanonical proof, the answer is that what makes a noncanonical proof a proof is that its function is to establish the possibility of canonical proof. This is just what such a proof consists in: it shows how to construct a canonical proof, or at least provides a demonstration that one must be available. To apply this model to the case of the missing umbrella, the idea is that we give the meaning of the statement 'My umbrella is in the bank' by laying down what is to count as an observation that it is true. Other methods of establishing the correctness of this statement count as such because they consist in arguments that observation must be possible, proofs that canonical proof can be had.

Though it seems to explain the two features of the example I highlighted, the model of a verificationist account of our understanding of mathematical statements is not applicable to ordinary empirical statements. The fundamental reason is the role in ordinary empirical thinking of grasp of a simple theory of perception and action. The reasoning which convinces us that the umbrella is in the bank does not, after all, make any reference whatever to my possible observations. Its parallel in mathematics would be a nonconstructive proof, which does not proceed by trying to show how to find a canonical proof of the conclusion or even that one must be available. What convinces us that observation of the umbrella in the bank must be possible is not anything internal to the reasoning involved at all. It is rather the conviction that the umbrella is in the bank, together with something that has no parallel in the mathematical case: grasp of a simple theory of perception and action.

This explains another phenomenon that has no parallel in the mathematical case: the fact that observation of the state of affairs may be impossible because no one was around at the time it happened and now it is too late. So, for example, it may be that although the umbrella is in the bank now, as I hasten toward it, by the time I get there, it will be too late, and I will never see it again. In mathematics, however, if a canonical proof is available, then a canonical proof is available, and it is never too late. The point is that we have no parallel in mathematics for our ordinary grasp of a simple theory of perception and action, which might explain why proof of a proposition is sometimes available and sometimes not. The upshot is that grasp of a simple theory is intrinsic to our understanding of what it is for an ordinary empirical proposition to be true. It is vital to our grasp of truth, because it controls our understanding of the variety of ways in which propositions may be established and their relations to one another.

Philosophers of an empiricist or pragmatist bent have often questioned our understanding of what seem to be distinctively realist aspects of spatial or temporal thinking that are used in the simple theory. What is right about this is that, as we saw, we certainly do have to assign causal significance to spatial and temporal notions. For example, if we say that an organism is representing events as *simultaneous,* we must be able to say how it gives causal meaning to the notion. Another thing that is right about empiricist or pragmatist critique is that very often the way in which a notion is given causal meaning is through direct connections with perception and action. The mistake is to suppose that this is the only way in which causal meaning can be assigned to spatial and temporal notions, as if there were no such thing as the reflective understanding of causation displayed in possession and use of a simple theory and, correlatively, in an understanding of the past.

As we saw when I described our basic conceptual repertoire, there is a certain systematicity in it. One has a range of perceptual identifications of particular objects and a range of conceptions of physical properties and can think of any of the objects as having any of the properties. One has a range of identifications of people and a range of ways of thinking of their psychological states and can think of any of the people as having any of the psychological properties. On one view, the existence of this systematicity in our thought is simply an empirical contingency (Fodor 1987). It reflects no deep norm in our thinking. What we have seen in this section is that the systematicity in our thought is inextricably linked to our grasp of a simple theory of perception and action and that this is intrinsic to our understanding of the truth or falsity of ordinary empirical statements. But this too may be held to be an empirical contingency and to reflect no deep norm.

Here we might compare the animals using the slope-centroid model in navigating around their environment that I described in section 1.3. These animals have no simple theory of perception and action, and their method of representation is not systematic in the way that ours is, though it is certainly structured. Correlatively, their understanding of the truth or falsity of their representations is quite different from ours. Indeed, it is a good question whether we need any distinction between the animal being warranted to depend on a representation and the representation actually being true. Whatever we say about this, it may be held that here too the notion of truth being used and the way in which representation is structured are simply empirical facts about the animal, with no deep normative status.

We can throw the issue here into relief and begin to see how difficult it is in the case of human conceptual thinking by considering a case in which the structure in content really is normative. For a simple example, consider a chess-playing computer, and suppose we disregard the impossibility of pawns being on their own back rank—the computer takes no explicit note of this fact. If the computer is to fulfill its function, it must be able to represent every square on the board, it must be able to represent every piece, and, with the proviso just noted, it must be able to represent any piece as on any square. This is not just an empirical fact about the computer; it is not, for example, just an artifact of the medium of computation that it happens to be using. It is a norm governing its representations. If the computer had a blind spot somewhere, that would evidently be a deficiency. What controls the ascription of content to the computer is that it has a tightly defined task to perform: it is supposed to play and win games. If it is to do this, it will have to be able to represent any piece as on any square. So its representations have to be systematic.

Does a parallel account apply to ordinary human thinking, so that it is not simply an empirical fact that it is systematic but is rather a normative condition on thought? It is not easy to see how to apply the parallel. The computer has a tightly defined task to perform, one defined by the intentions of its programmer. It is sometimes supposed that evolutionary teleology stands to biological representation somewhat as the intentions of the programmer stand to the representations of the computer. Helpful though it often is, that idea cannot work here. The idea can only work if evolutionary teleology is allowed to define some point for the system. But human thinking is, as Fodor (1983) put it, "general purpose." There is no single task that it has to perform. So there is no way in which we could derive norms governing the systematicity of thinking from consideration of "the function" it has to fulfill. It might be said that in thinking, we use linguistic tokens of various types, and that an evolutionary story can be told about the function of each type of token (Millikan 1984). But we could give such an account while leaving it as an empirical matter that our thinking happens to be systematic.

There is another way in which the parallel with the chess-playing computer lets us down. If the computer is to function properly, it must be able to represent any piece as on any square. This does not of itself mean that there must be any particular causal structure in its grasp of representations, so long as it achieves the upshot, by whatever gerrymandering, that it can represent any piece as on any square, this is all that is needed. But the idea that humans possess concepts does not just require that there should be a certain pattern in the totality of thoughts that someone understands. It requires that there should be a causal structure in the grasp of thoughts that is responsible for the total pattern in which thoughts are understood. The model of the chess-playing computer gives us no indication of how one might derive a need for such causal structure as a content-governing norm.

Let us ponder the sense in which ordinary human thinking is general purpose. An animal can have a variety of wants and desires, and it may have some central organization, that is, the structure of its cognition may include a central system that can subserve any of those wants and desires. Now the mere fact that a creature's cognition has this structure does not mean that it possesses concepts; in other words, it does not guarantee that its thought will be systematic in the way in which human thought is. Animals using the slope-centroid model are centrally organized and have a variety of wants and desires, but they do not possess concepts.

Human thinking is general purpose in a much stronger sense. Humans do not just have a variety of wants and desires. They can take things into their own hands and determine for themselves what their wants and desires will be. It is not just that they have second-order desires: desires to have certain desires. One can have a particular conception of one's own life, what its shape is, how it has gone so far, and how one wants the rest of it to go. And this conception is always up for discussion and criticism and revision. Human thinking, then, is general purpose in the very strong sense that it can be bent to the needs of a conception of how to live and used in articulating and criticizing such a conception. That is why it is hard to find a norm governing human thinking as such that could be used to derive a normative status for the systematicity of thought. There is no single, externally defined function that human thinking has to fulfill. And it is not even that there is a range of functions that human thinking has. Rather, each of us can determine for himself or herself what the guiding lights of his or her life will be.[1]

Having seen why the problem of finding a normative status for the systematicity of thought is so intractable, we have also solved it. What is responsible for its normative status is the fact that, as I began this chapter by remarking, a precondition of self-consciousness, of a dynamic grasp of one's own causal structure, is that one possesses concepts and that one's thinking is therefore systematic. The normative status of the systematicity is owed to the fact that one must grasp one's own causal structure to form a conception of how to live, and consequently to be a free agent at all.

I began this section by remarking that the systematicity in our thought is inextricably bound to our understanding of the truth or falsity of ordinary empirical statements. If the way of finding a normative status for systematicity that I have just proposed is correct, then it also ought to apply to our understanding of truth and falsity. To this issue I now turn.

6.3   Realism

Realism is often characterized as the doctrine that a statement may be true even though it is in principle impossible for us to tell that it is true.[2] This does not constitute a positive analysis of our ordinary notion of truth; it simply puts a condition on it. The problem with this formulation—that a statement may be true though it is in principle impossible for us to tell that it is—is that it talks about what is or is not possible, whereas what we really care about is the basis of the possibility. This is a recurring problem with modal formulations of philosophical views. For example, consider the idea that materialism about the mind is the view it is impossible for two people to have all their physical characteristics in common but differ in their mental states. This is widely felt to be unsatisfactory as a definition of materialism, because what we want to know is why this is impossible; the doctrine of materialism should ground the supervenience claim, not be identified with it. Or again, analyses of causation in counterfactual terms often seem unsatisfactory because what matters for causation are not the various counterfactual possibilities themselves but the real-world relation that grounds these possibilities. In the case of realism, once again, what matters is not the truth of the modal claim but the ground of the possibility. What matters for realism is how a statement could be true even though we cannot tell that it is.

I can dramatize the point by remarking that even an antirealist can accept the modal claim that a statement could be true without our being able to tell that it is. This would still be an antirealist view, so long as there is an antirealist basis for the modal claim. For example, one could hold that reality is a human construction, while maintaining that it is not point by point a human construction. It might be that overall the world is a human construction but that as an artifact of the general construction process used, some statements have their truth values determined, even though we in principle have no way of finding out which truth values we have determined them to have (Kreisel 1969).

Moreover, even a realist might deny the modal claim, that is, deny that it is in principle possible for a statement to be true without our being able to recognize that it is. This can still be a realist view; everything depends on the reason why the modal claim is rejected. For example, someone who is a realist about the environment might hold that we cannot think of "the mind" in isolation from the environment in which it is embedded. On this view, the mind is plastic; it is open to being shaped by whatever surroundings it finds itself in, for the mind is just a kind of openness to the world. Pursuing this highly externalist conception of the mind, one could hold that it is sufficiently susceptible to shaping by its environment that it can find out about any environment in which it is located. This view can hold that the plasticity of the mind means that any truth can be known, but it is not thereby an antirealist position. The claim that there is a match between our cognitive powers and the world is here based not on the idea that the world is constructed by us but rather on the idea that the mind is shaped by the world.

What we need is a distinctively realist way of describing the ground of the possibility that a statement may be true even though we cannot recognize it as such. On the face of it, though, what we need here is something relatively elementary. We need the idea that a statement may be true even though no one was appropriately positioned to observe its truth. We need the idea that the reason why we did not find out about something, or that we could not affect a particular outcome, was some limitation on our own powers. For example, something may have happened, and the reason why no one found out about it may be simply that no one was there at the time, no one was so positioned as to observe it happening. Or again, it may be that no one was so positioned as to be able to affect what was happening. This kind of point appeals to our reflective understanding of our own place in the world. It exploits our grasp of a simple theory of perception and action. This theory explains our perceptions as the joint upshot of the way things are in the world and the way things are with us, and it explains the effects of our actions as the joint consequences of our bodily movements and the way things were around us to begin with. On the face of it, our grasp of this simple theory of perception and action provides us with a classically realist picture of the relation between ourselves and our environment. On the one hand, there is the world, waiting to be perceived or acted on; on the other, there is the subject, perceiving and acting on more or less extensive regions of the world in ways that depend on his own powers and position. Despite its realism, this picture is relatively innocent; indeed, it is the picture an innocent would have of our relation to the world. Appeal to our grasp of this simple theory identifies the realism in our ordinary thinking; it identifies what seems so evidently mistaken about antirealism. The use of the simple theory immediately makes apparent the need to distinguish between the truth of a proposition and its being warrantedly assertible. In one kind of case, the perception that things are so is explained jointly by the fact that things are so and by one's being appropriately positioned. But the truth of a proposition is only one factor in one's being warranted in asserting it. And this causal analysis of one's being warranted in forming the judgement also makes it intelligible that the upshot, the warranted assertibility of the proposition, could be brought about by something other than the thing's being so. Of course, if things are so and one's own perception of them as so is explained in part by that, then other people may also have perceptions of them as so, explained in similar ways. So communication about a shared world is possible; swapping memories about what we did and saw together, so long ago, is possible. Continuing articulation of what we do here is what elaborates on the point of our concept of truth, without in any way offering a reduction or analysis of it.

There is a simple problem for any antirealism about the ordinary world of things around us, any view on which the world is somehow a construct of ours. On such a view, there is no more to the world than is possible for us to discover. For the world is simply constituted by our capacities to find out about it. But if we regard ourselves as humans, creatures of bounded intelligence in a backwater of the Milky Way, then it seems at best an astonishing contingency that there is no more to the world than is possible for us to find out. Why should there be this match between the complexity of the universe and the complexity of our capacity to find things out? How can we be sure that the universe is not just a shade too difficult for us, or perhaps even orders of magnitude too difficult for us? Suppose, though, that scientists advise us that our minds are indeed powerful enough to find out all there is to know, and suppose we believe them. Even if this contingency holds, it does not give the antirealist what he wants. The antirealist wants to insist that there is some deep necessity to the match between the world and our capacity to find out about it. But as long as we think of ourselves as human beings, this result seems quite incredible. How can any amount of philosophical argument turn something that is obviously at best an astonishing contingency into a necessity? It is with something like this thought that most people approach antirealist argument, and because of this thought, antirealism seems so evidently mistaken. In explaining the match, the antirealist can hardly appeal to the externalist conception of the mind as plastic, which I described above. But neither does it seem possible to reconcile the necessity of the match with the conception of ourselves as ordinary humans, awash with limitations. The only way in which the antirealist can hope to persuade is by inclining his audience to regard the "we" who can in principle know anything as a kind of vanishing point of metaphysical inquiry, a limiting point of the world rather than an element in it. But then one simply loses one's grip on who "we" are; one can no longer think of oneself as a human being, for example, rather than as a kind of vanishing point, a limit of inquiry, like the origin of the visual field. One loses any conception of oneself at all; one no longer has any consciousness of self. A similar point could be made about pragmatism, understood as the view that there is no more to the way things are than is exhausted by our capacities for intervention, and its relation to realism.

We have already looked in some detail at one source of the oscillation between the two views of the self here, namely, the oscillation between the first person thought of as a token-reflexive, governed by the rule that any token of it refers to whoever produced it, versus the first person as functioning on analogy with a perceptual demonstrative. The fact that the first person is a token-reflexive means that its use to refer does not depend on one's having an accurate conception of the thing to which it refers. If one fails to grasp fully the point that the first person is a token-reflexive, though, and has in mind the use of a perceptual demonstrative as the model of reference, then it will seem that the use of the first person to refer must depend on one's having an accurate conception of something, but when one asks what that thing is, the only reply one can come up with is that it cannot be identified with any constituent of the world. The picture changes once we give full weight to the point that the first person is a token-reflexive. For then we have to ask about the relation between the rule of reference for the term and the use made of it, its conceptual role.

As we saw, if one is to use the first person according to the token-reflexive rule, one must use it with psychological predicates in a way that shows sensitivity to the two dimensions of one's causal structure at the the level of one's psychological properties. This involves being able to think of one's later psychological states as causally depending on one's earlier psychological states. The fact that one is thinking of one's causal connectedness over time does not mean that one's first-person thought is not engaged with the spatiotemporal framework. On the contrary. If we ask what makes the difference between merely thinking of oneself as having a sequence of psychological states and thinking of one's later states as causally depending on earlier ones, the answer we get is this. Someone who thinks of his later states as causally depending on earlier ones grasps the role of interactions in producing the later ones. He has the idea that the upshot of an interaction depends partly on the nature of the thing with which he is interacting and partly on his own prior condition. The principal interactions we have to consider here involve precisely those of the simple theory of perception and action: the crucial idea is that perceptual interactions are marking interactions, leaving memories as traces. The problem now is to determine whether it is possible for the antirealist to think of the self in this way, to use the first person according to these norms of its conceptual role. Specifically, I want to ask whether it is possible for someone who takes an antirealist view of the past to use the first person in this way.

Using the first person in this way demands that one think of memory as being, as I shall put it, "stepwise" or "dependent." One thinks of one's autobiographical memories as produced by earlier perceptions of one's surroundings. One does not think of memory as constituting an independent type of epistemic access to one's surroundings. It can function to give one knowledge of one's past life because it depends on other ways of knowing about one's circumstances; in particular, it depends on knowing about one's environment through perception. In the last chapter we will see that thinking of memory in this way involves thinking of memory as of the same world that one encounters from time to time, and we will consider whether this conception of a single world on which we have various temporal perspectives is ultimately available to the antirealist. The argument of this book is that the norms governing distinctively human conceptual thought, as opposed to other types of representation, are set by the demands of self-consciousness and its interwoveness with the spatiotemporal framework, and that these norms governing conceptual thought demand a realist view of the past.

7

The Realism of Memory

7.1 The Opposition to Realism

Memory seems to be a way of spanning temporal perspectives, a description of the world formulated at one time used when describing it at another. So, for example, if I am asked to recall the events of the evening of 17 March 1990, I summon up the description I formulated then and, with appropriate changes in tense, use it to say how things were then. This procedure assumes that there is a single temporal reality onto which all one's various temporal perspectives face, so that the judgements I make at one time can be the basis of knowledge at a later time. This characteristic of memory brings our ordinary reliance on it into conflict with any view which opposes realism about the past. My aim in this chapter is to explain more fully the conflict between memory and antirealism, to show that a kind of realism is engraved in our memories. I begin with some remarks on the rationale for antirealism about the past and then go on to discuss the conflict with our ordinary reliance on memory.

The motive for antirealism about the past has traditionally been a desire to understand hypotheses about particular past happenings in a way that does not make it forever impossible to find out whether they are true.[1] It received extended discussion by the American pragmatists. There is, for example, a good statement of the point in C. I. Lewis 1956:

The assumption that the past is intrinsically verifiable means that at any date after the happening of an event, there is always something, which at least is conceivably possible of experience, by means of which it can be known. Let us call these items its "effects." The totality of such effects quite obviously constitute all of the object that is knowable. To separate the effects from the object is, thus, to transform it into some incognizable *ding an sich*. (150–153)

Here Lewis was drawing on a tradition of resistance to realism about the past begun by William James and Charles S. Peirce.[2] This tradition was robustly maintained by A. J. Ayer:

For my own part, I do not find anything excessively paradoxical in the view that propositions about the past are rules for the prediction of those "historical" experiences which are commonly said to verify them, and I do not see how else our knowledge of the past is to be analyzed. And I suspect, moreover, that those who object to our pragmatic treatment of history are really basing their objections on a tacit, or explicit, assumption that the past is somehow "objectively there" to be corresponded to—that it is "real" in the metaphysical sense of the term. . . . It is clear that such an assumption is not a genuine hypothesis.[3]

This passage makes explicit the characteristic thesis of antirealism about the past: that understanding statements about particular past events is a matter of being able to verify or falsify them. So understood, a past-tense statement is true if there is evidence presently available for it. This can be qualified a little, since someone who is an antirealist about the past should surely allow that further evidence might turn up in the future. And if he has some sophistication about the notion of evidence being used, he ought to insist that what matters is evidence that we can now recognize as such, since what moves him is reflection on how we presently understand our words. So we can put the antirealist thesis like this: a statement in the past tense is true just if there is available, now or in the future, evidence for the statement that we can presently recognize as such.[4]

In this chapter my interest is in the way in which our ordinary reliance on memory already stands opposed to any such view. I want to ask just how much of a commitment to realism about the past there is in the way we use memory. So I will set aside some natural objections to antirealism about the past, though I am sympathetic to simple outrage. For example, it might be held to be a consequence of the Second Law of Thermodynamics that there is less information about the past available at one time than was available at an earlier time. On the face of it, the antirealist's thesis means that there cannot be more to the past than there is present or future evidence for, but this seems to run counter to the Second Law. Or again, it might be held that the antirealist has to give a primacy to tensed locutions that they cannot bear; in particular, that Special Relativity is inconsistent with any weight being put on the notion of the present, or now.[5] This response holds that antirealism about the past depends on some privileged status being given to the evidence available now or in the future. But, the response continues, what is happening now, what happened earlier, and what will happen later depend on our choice of a frame of reference, and it is not credible that an arbitrary frame of reference could have such significance. As I said, I will not be pursuing these objections here. I want rather to look at the way in which we ordinarily rely on memory and to ask whether this way involves any commitment to realism. For there is something very distinctive about the way in which the antirealist opposes realism about the past. He holds that temporal reality must always be described from some temporal perspective. Consequently, he holds that the perspective from which reality must be apprehended shifts over time.

In contrast, consider, for example, an opponent of mathematical realism, who supposes that what makes mathematical truths true are deep contingencies about human nature, about what we can or cannot imagine or conceive.[6] Someone who takes this line would not say that each of us does in fact occupy different mathematical perspectives at different times. On the contrary, the point of insisting on the depth of the contingencies of human nature in which mathematical truth is rooted is to insist that we cannot simply shake off the mathematical perspective we occupy. Someone opposed to realism about the past, though, has to acknowledge that a single person will, at different times, occupy quite different temporal perspectives. For the antirealist, this is just a way of saying that persons endure. And memory seems to be the way in which persons span different perspectives.

7.2   Truth-Value Links

Memory depends on the existence of links between the truth values of differently tensed judgements made at different times. For example, suppose that today I judge, 'There is a commotion in the village'. If tomorrow I remember today's events, I will have to express the memory by saying, 'Yesterday, there was a commotion in the village'. This exploits the existence of a link between the truth values of the two judgements. If one is true, so too is the other. Memory could not give us knowledge of the past if it were not for these truth-value links. Grasp of these links is, indeed, part of our ordinary understanding of tense itself. It is part of an understanding of tense that one realize that time is, as it were, on the move. If, having once formed the judgement 'It is raining', I woodenly held on to the present-tense formulation, so that I could see no way of giving up my tendency to keep repeating, 'It is raining', without acknowledging that my original judgement was mistaken, I would not have understood the way in which the tensed temporal indicators work. Neither would I have grasped the way tense works if I thought that having made a present-tense judgement, I had, as it were, shot my bolt, and that this has no implications for the kinds of judgements I ought to make at later times. This would mean that my present-tense judgements left no trace on my propositional states. What one needs to have is a capacity to keep track of time, however rudimentary, so that one can systematically manipulate the tensed temporal indicators that figure in one's judgements, as time passes. (It may be, incidentally, that one can use tense even though one is seriously amnesic and unable to use this primitive way of keeping track of time, provided that one can still use, for example, a calendar and clock to pin down one's tensed judgements for later reference.)

It might be held that our reliance on memory does not require dependence on the truth-value links, because we simply lay down that memory of yesterday's rain constitutes evidence for there having been rain then, and this is all there is to be said. But this view does not do justice to the complexity of the way in which we ordinarily use and criticize memory and the different ways in which we suppose things can go wrong with it. In ordinary memory we exploit an inherited mechanism attuned to the rhythms of the environment and our bodies, a mechanism that can go wrong. Consider, for example, waking up and recalling the events of the previous day. The shift from having been willing to judge, yesterday evening, 'A thunderstorm is in progress', to judging, in the morning, 'There was a thunderstorm yesterday evening', is not achieved by inductive reasoning, using collateral data to establish just how long ago the thing happened.

Rather, keeping track of time here is done partly by manipulating the tensed indicators. This kind of cognitive dynamics can break down independently of other aspects of memory and is assessed as operating properly or not by appealing to the truth-value links. So Rip van Winkle, for example, has gone wrong in the way that he keeps track of time, though otherwise his memory is perfectly sound. In pinpointing what has gone wrong in his case, we take the truth-value links for granted and use them as yardsticks by which to assess Rip's performance. We do not regard memory as somehow trumping the truth-value links: it depends on them, and we use them in criticizing it.[7]

A question often pressed against the antirealist is whether he can acknowledge these truth-value links.[8] The problem is that evidence available at one time may not be available at a later time: it may be permanently destroyed. So it may be that when a judgement is made, evidence for it is then available, but by the time a later, truth-value linked judgement is made, all evidence for that judgement has been permanently destroyed. At first it may seem, then, as though the antirealist would be committed to regarding the first judgement as true and the second as not true, which thus violates the rule that they have the same truth value.

There is, in fact, no immediate problem for the antirealist here once we make a sharp separation between the time at which a judgement is made and the time, the present, at which which we are inquiring into its truth value. Let us go back to the formulation of antirealism given earlier, that is, that any concrete judgement, made at *any* time, is true only if there *now* is (or subsequently will be) evidence for that judgement. Suppose that two judgements made at different times are truth-value-linked in the way I have been discussing. Then anything that is present evidence for one is present evidence for the other. So they are bound to have the same truth-value.

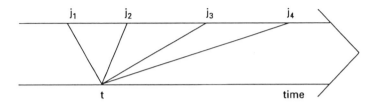

Figure 7.1
The figure shows the distinction between the time at which a particular judgement is made and the time, the present, relative to which it is evaluated for truth or falsity. Truth-value-linked judgements j_1 through j_4 made at different times have the same truth value when evaluated relative to the same time of evaluation t.

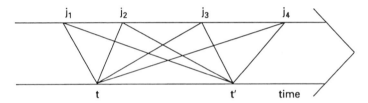

Figure 7.2
Here j_1 through j_4 are truth-value-linked judgements, and t and t' are our times of evaluation. Relative to t, j_1 to j_4 all receive the same truth value. Relative to t', they again all receive the same evaluation. But there is no guarantee that they receive the same value relative to t as they do relative to t'.

We can diagram the situation as in figure 7.1. Here j_1 through j_4 are truth-value-linked concrete judgements, and t is the time, the present, at which we are inquiring into their truth values. This diagram makes graphic the separation of the time at which the judgement is made from the time of evaluation. Given this separation, it is obvious that the antirealist can secure the truth-value links.

However, given this way of explaining his position, another problem immediately arises. For we can generalize the notion of a time of evaluation, and consider what happens when we look at the evaluations that judgements receive relative to different times of evaluation, not just the present. Since evidence may be permanently destroyed, it would seem that a single concrete judgement can receive the value true relative to one time of evaluation but the value false relative to a later time of evaluation, when all the evidence has been destroyed. We can diagram the situation as in figure 7.2. Here j_1 through j_4 are truth-value-linked concrete judgements, and t and t' are our times of evaluation. Relative to t, j_1 through j_4 all receive the same truth value. Relative to t', they again all receive the same evaluation. What is not guaranteed is that they receive the same value relative to t as they do relative to t'.

The general structure of this point is common to any antirealist view of a given area that holds that the area has to be understood in terms of its relation to a particular perspective. The question is simply whether there cannot be other perspectives on that same area. What is extraordinary about antirealism about the past is the urgency with which this issue comes up. For since the antirealist recognizes that he himself is an enduring thing and can remember his earlier positions as well as anticipate what views he will later hold, he has to acknowledge that he has occupied and will occupy perspectives other than his current one.

It is instructive to compare the position of the antirealist here with, for example, the position of someone who holds an anthropocentric view of mathematical truth. On this view, mathematical truths are rooted in deep contingencies of human nature. Suppose we ask how this view copes with the necessity of mathematical truths. We want to be able to say, for example, that $2 + 3$ would have been 5 even if human nature had been quite otherwise than it is, even if the deep contingencies of human nature in which mathematical truth is grounded had not been realized. Someone who takes this view must insist on a distinction between the world with respect to which a mathematical statement is being evaluated for truth or falsity and the world in which we are carrying out this evaluation. The latter world is the actual world, the world in which we find our mathematical perspective. On this view, then, the evaluation of '2 + 3 = 5' with respect to any possible world will depend on what our human nature is in the actual world. This is what the anthropocentrism consists in. Given the designation of a particular world as actual, this view secures the necessity of mathematical truths by ensuring that they receive the same evaluation with respect to all possible worlds. There is, though, a further question for the anthropocentric view. This is whether mathematical truths are not necessary also in a different sense, namely, that they are true no matter which world is designated as actual. On the face of it, this is exactly what the anthropocentric view denies. Now so far, the situation of the antirealist about mathematics is formally exactly parallel to that of the antirealist about the past. What is not parallel in the mathematical case is the role that memory plays for the antirealist about the past. For it seems to force recognition of connections between the evaluations made from different perspectives. It would, in contrast, be quite difficult to force a sufficiently hard-headed antirealist about mathematics to acknowledge that there are connections between the evaluations made when different worlds are designated as actual.

In general, there are recognizable antirealist types of response to this type of question. One response is to say that it depends on supposing that we can have a 'sideways on' view of our practice, from which we can see that our own perspective is simply one among many. But, it may be held, this 'sideways on' view is impossible: we are always operating within our practice and cannot somehow transcend our conceptual apparatus. So figure 7.2 cannot be understood as giving a 'sideways on' view of the present as one time among many.[9] The figure has to be interpreted from our present perspective. Alternatively, the antirealist may give some abstract acknowledgement of perspectives other than his own but maintain that there is a kind of incommensurability between the different viewpoints, so that from one's own perspective, one cannot really understand the thought of the other. I now want to consider how these types of response apply to antirealism about the past. In particular, what are the implications for our ordinary reliance on memory? Consider a case in which a concrete judgement receives different evaluations relative to different times of evaluation. For example, suppose that the colonel loses his temper with the butler but that a year later all evidence for this having happened has vanished forever. So the judgement 'The colonel lost his temper with the butler' receives different evaluations relative to different times. Is this situation tolerable? If the judgement is univocal, surely it is not, for when one makes a judgement, one is aiming at truth, and one loses all grasp of what one is about if there is no notion of truth to state what one is aiming at.[10] If the antirealist is to preserve even a semblance of our ordinary procedures in making judgements, he will have to maintain that we aim at securing truth relative to the present as the time of evaluation: we are sensitive to the present availability of evidence for our judgements. But then, on the face of it, at different times we must be aiming at different targets, different conceptions of truth, in making our judgements. Since in memory a judgement formed at one time is used again at a later time, even though, on this account, the activity of judgement has different goals at different times, we have to pursue the question of what view of memory the antirealist can give.

7.3   The Stepwise Conception of Memory

The real conflict here is between the antirealist's view of the past and what we might call the "stepwise" or "dependent" character of memory. In this section I want to spend some time describing this aspect of memory. The feature I have in mind is a characteristic that memory shares with testimony. Testimony depends on there being ways other than testimony of finding out how things are. If you tell me something, the possibility of my finding out how things are by believing you depends on your having known that thing already. Perhaps you too found out only by being told, but at some point someone must have relied on some way of finding out how things are other than testimony. Testimony is not an independent channel to the truth; testimony depends on there being ways of finding things out other than testimony. Memory also has this stepwise character. It is, as it were, the testimony of one's earlier self. In one central type of case, one forms a judgement, perhaps on the basis of perception, and the status of that original judgement as knowledge is essential to the epistemic status of one's subsequent memory judgement. The groundedness of the memory judgement depends on the groundedness of the original judgement. Of course, a memory judgement need not trace back to some prior judgement. It may be that one had some information channel to the truth—perhaps one saw the murder but at the time did not trust one's senses, or perhaps one was told about it but did not trust one's informant—and only formed one's memory judgement later on being assured of the credibility of one's senses or of one's informant. Or perhaps one simply did not notice at the time and realized what was happening only on recollecting the scene.

Incidentally, it may be that knowledge of one's own past psychological states need not be stepwise in this way. Consider, for example, knowledge of one's past emotions and moods. This characteristically has as its most primitive form the articulation of one's state: there is no knowledge of the state prior to one's giving it linguistic shape. This is not to say that one's characterization of the state is incorrigible. Indeed, in this kind of case the possibilities for further qualification and amplification seem almost endless. But there is no direct, non-linguistic access to the state itself, which one is merely trying to hit off verbally. Rather, the capacity for verbal articulation is the whole story about one's epistemic access to the state. And plainly one need not—indeed, one often cannot—verbally articulate one's current psychological states. One's heart may be too full for words, and knowledge of exactly what one's mood and emotions were may come only afterward. In this type of case, one has epistemic access to a past state that does not depend on one's having actually had any earlier epistemic access to the state.

As we have seen, even in the case of perceptual judgements, it is too strong to demand that the input itself must have been knowledge for the memory to be knowledge. It might be, for instance, that one rejected the original sense impression as illusory but later came to see that one had no good reason for the rejection, so one comes to trust the sense impression. In this case the upshot can plainly be knowledge. But there must be some epistemic conditions on the character of the input. One approach is to distinguish between "ground-floor" and "reflective" conditions on knowledge. Among the ground-floor conditions, we might include suitable causal connectedness between the remembered state and the sense impression, or whether the sense impression "tracks" the state, in Robert Nozick's sense (1981, pt. 3). We can also include demands to the effect that the type of state in question should be one of which one could acquire observational knowledge, or that there should be some kind of "match" between the method of investigation being used and the type of content in question. Thus, to use Christopher Peacocke's example (1986, chap. 10), even if one's perceptions of water are tracking whether something is H_2O, this is not enough for them to yield noninferential, observational knowledge that H_2O is present. This is so even though similar noninferential observation could give one knowledge of the presence of water.[11] In contrast to these ground-floor constraints, there are reflective constraints on knowledge, which have to do with the thinker's reflections on the process by which he is forming his beliefs. For example, we might hold that knowledge requires the thinker to have some reason for using the methods of inquiry he does, rather than any others.

I want to propose that for episodic memory to constitute knowledge, the original perception or judgement formed by the subject must meet the ground-floor constraints, whatever they are. The reflective constraints, however, need not be met by the original representation. Intuitively, the point is that any shortfall in meeting reflective constraints can be made up later by the thinker. For example, if knowledge does require that one should have some reason to think that one's methods of inquiry are correct, this reason need not have been available at the time the original representation was formed; it is enough if one grasps the reason later. This marks a contrast between memory and inference. In the case of an ordinary inference, the argument can yield knowledge only if the premises themselves are known; the inputs to the process must be in every way epistemically sound. In inference there is not enough of a gap between the input and the output contexts to leave room for the possibility of reflective conditions being made up en route. The distinction between ground-floor and reflective conditions does seem to mark a point of analogy between memory and testimony, though. For testimony to yield knowledge, the input to the process must meet the ground-floor conditions on knowledge, but it does seem plausible that deficiencies in the reflective conditions on the part of the testifier can be made up by the recipient of the knowledge.

Incidentally, I have been concerned with the stepwise character only of episodic, or more particularly autobiographical, memories.[12] Whether we can say that nonepisodic, or semantic, memory must in general be stepwise is the central philosophical question raised by the idea of innate knowledge. If there can be innate knowledge, then of course the evolutionary forces that shaped the inherited brainstate must be epistemically reliable. But this is not to say that the subject could ever have had non-memory-based access to the information. Just for this reason, one might want to insist that there cannot be innate knowledge possessed by a subject, that "innate knowledge" must always be a subpersonal characteristic of a brain system, such as an input or motor system. Yet whatever we say on this issue, there are many areas in which the operation of semantic memory is manifestly stepwise. One must have picked up knowledge from one's teachers, for example, if one's memories of what one learned at school are to constitute knowledge: the ground-floor constraints must have been met. And if one's memory of the color of strawberries, for example, is to constitute knowledge, it must be derived from perceptions that meet the ground-floor constraints indicated above.

Russell was unusual in that he attempted to deny the stepwise character even of episodic memory. In *The Problems of Philosophy* (1967, chaps. 5, 11), he takes the view that memory of past objects is a form of acquaintance with them that is just as direct and immediate as perceptual acquaintance. Memory is exactly on a par with perception: it in no way depends on it. It is not a matter of having a present image in the mind; rather, it is a kind of epistemic contact with the past that one can use to control and correct one's imagery. And it is an epistemic contact with the past unmediated by one's past perceptions; it reaches directly to the past objects.[13] Russell restricted acquaintance to our sense data and our mental states and possibly ourselves. His view here thus inherits some of the plausibility of the position that memory of one's past psychological states need not be stepwise, as I remarked above. Consider, however, what would go wrong if we retained Russell's insistence on the nonstepwise character of memory while expanding the scope of acquaintance to include middle-sized physical objects. The difficulty with the idea of such a subject becomes apparent when we reflect on the role of the stepwise character of memory in providing for one's sense of one's past location and actions. What one can remember, we ordinarily think, depends in part on where one was, whether one was in a position to find out about what was happening. Someone whose knowledge of the past was direct, in the sense that it did not depend on his having had other ways of finding out, would not have this central way of finding out about his own past position. His access to the past would range indiscriminately over the past and would not depend on his past location. For one's past situation matters only because one is relying on one's past possession of other channels to the truth than memory. Without the stepwise conception of memory, one loses the right to say, for example, 'I must have been in the town center this afternoon, because I remember seeing Carfax', or 'I seem to remember seeing Big Ben last Thursday, but that can't be right, because I was nowhere near Big Ben last Thursday'.

Again, the stepwise character of memory is put to work in our ordinary ways of supporting or criticizing particular memory judgements. This is despite the feature of our ordinary thinking that we do not keep track of our justifications for the beliefs we have. One may remember that it rained in Oxford last Tuesday without remembering how one found out about it: whether one saw the rain, heard it, or was told about it. But in general, we adhere to what Harman (1986) calls the "Principle of Positive Undermining": that one should stop believing p whenever one positively believes one's reasons for believing p are no good. The way in which we implement this principle in the case of memories concerning particular past states of affairs involves the idea that I can find out whether I was in a position to know about a past state of affairs independently of finding out whether the state did obtain. So, for example, I may realize that I could not have discovered whether it was raining in Oxford last Tuesday because I was, at the time and subsequently, in Bombay and quite out of contact with anyone who might have known. I can realize this without inquiring into whether or not it did actually rain last Tuesday, and in this case I have no option but to suspend judgement on whether it rained in Oxford then. Here our practice puts to work the stepwise character of memory and its connection with one's knowledge of one's own past location in criticizing a particular memory judgement.

I can give a preliminary formulation of the problem that this dependent character of memory presents for the antirealist by remarking that there is an epistemological constraint on any account of truth such as his. The constraint is that it must be possible to represent our interest in knowledge as a product solely of our interest in truth. If this is not possible, if we can explain our interest in knowledge only as a product of our interest in truth together with our interest in something else, then we have failed to explain the point of our concept of knowledge. For it will then be obscure why we should not abandon the quest for knowledge, letting go the something else, whatever it is, and concentrate solely on the pursuit of truth.[14] Suppose that I now have evidence about a particular past event: I remember that the butler was polishing a revolver, for example. The dependent character of memory means that this judgement does not count as knowledge unless I make it in virtue of my having had some access to that polishing, otherwise than through memory. What is required is that, for example, I saw him doing it. But on the antirealist's account, the truth of the present judgement consists just in the present or future availability of evidence for it. If I am aiming only at truth, then this is all that concerns me. The past availability of evidence is beside the point. My interest in truth requires only that I should assure myself of the present or future availability of evidence. If my interest in knowledge requires in addition that I should have had evidence for the judgement, then my interest in knowledge cannot be represented solely as a product of my interest in truth. For truth does not require that I should have had informational access in the past. But this point needs more discussion.

7.4   Incommensurability

The antirealist about the past has a particularly sharp problem to face when he considers what his philosophical views will be in the future, in a year's time, say. It is all very well for him to say that all that there is to the past is given by the evidence we have, now or in the future. A year from now he will presumably use the same form of words as he does now to express his philosophical views. So a year from now he will say, 'All there is to things having been so a year ago is the present or future availability of evidence that things were so'. But even if we were to agree that this is how things might seem in a year's time, at the moment it seems patently obvious that things are not so. What is happening now is one thing; whether the evidence for its having happened endures or is destroyed is something else. We can hardly accept that we are now living in a twilight zone, which is constituted by the future availability of evidence that things were thus and so. It is not as if we would have any promise that things would be any better in a year's time: we would be in exactly the same kind of twilight zone.

The antirealist may reply that this depends on supposing that it is one and the same world that is apprehended from all these various perspectives. In fact, he may say, there is an incommensurability between the different viewpoints, and from his own viewpoint he cannot really understand the thoughts of the other.

How can the antirealist motivate this claim of incommensurability? For an antirealist, grasp of what would make a statement true consists in presently having a capacity to recognize current or future states of affairs as evidence for the statement. A pragmatist approach would put the point a little differently: it consists in one's presently having an ability to respond appropriately to present or future evidence for the statement. Any such capacity, whether described in verificationist or pragmatist terms, will have to draw on an immense complex of facts about the subject: all his various propensities for evaluating of different types of judgment. Among other things, the capacity will depend on which particular things the subject can remember, a totality that it may be impossible to spell out completely. At some future time, when he has forgotten some of what he now remembers, the subject may be quite incapable of recapturing his present state. His present complex of evaluative propensities will by then have been lost forever. This of itself is not quite enough to establish the incommensurability of the judgements apprehended at different times. For it would still be open to say that we can give a high-level characterization of the content of a judgement that determines, for each possible surrounding range of auxiliary beliefs, what would constitute verification of the judgement. A grasp of content at this level of characterization would remain constant over time, despite changes in one's auxiliary beliefs. Given a particular judgement made now, one could, in a general kind of way, know in a year's time how one understood it earlier, because one can grasp the idea of there having been available, a year ago or subsequently, what would have been recognizable a year ago as evidence for it. We obtain the full force of the incommensurability thesis when we deny the possibility of any such high-level grasp of the content of a judgement and insist instead that understanding is just having the ability to recognize verifications as verifications. This really does give us a view on which the antirealist cannot grasp the judgement in the same way at different times; we have to acknowledge that it is not the same reality that is apprehended from different perspectives.

In Dummett's paper "The Reality of the Past" (1978), the final move made by the realist against the antirealist is as follows: Consider once again a statement such as, 'The colonel lost his temper with the butler', for which evidence is now available but for which all evidence will in a year's time have been permanently destroyed. The antirealist must now agree that the statement is true absolutely, but he must also acknowledge that a year hence he will maintain that the statement is not true absolutely. And he must agree that he will be correct in doing this. Dummett (1978) remarks that the antirealist "can hardly pretend that he will not say this, nor can he hope for much respect for his views if he denies that he will be correct in saying it." A year hence the antirealist can use the same form of words that he now uses to convince himself that, as he will then put it, a statement in the past tense is true only if there is available "now" (that is, a year hence) or subsequently evidence for the judgement that can "now" be recognized as such. So a year hence he will maintain that the judgement is not true absolutely, there being no evidence available for it, then or subsequently. If he maintains that he will be wrong to say this, it can only be because there is something wrong with the argument he will then be using to convince himself of his antirealist position, which is just the same as the form of words he is now using. In this situation, then, the antirealist's own views seem to commit him to inconsistency. At different times, he ascribes and denies absolute truth to one and the same concrete judgement.

The response made by Dummett's antirealist is that "he will not in a year's time mean the same by 'absolutely true' as he now means by it: indeed, he cannot by any means at all now express the meaning which he will attach to the phrase in a year's time." So the threat of diachronic inconsistency is to be met by claiming that the uses of the phrase 'absolutely true' at different times are incommensurable.

Wright (1987c) maintains that Dummett's antirealist is here "open to a simple dilemma." He asks, "Does his position permit the reconstruction of some sort of general notion of diachronic inconsistency, or does it not? If it does not, then . . . what account are we to give of the growth of human knowledge . . . ? But if some sort of notion of diachronic inconsistency can be saved, the task will still remain of showing that the . . . clash . . . does not obtain between his present and his later, and earlier, opinions." The reason for reinstating some notion of diachronic inconsistency is, then, to provide an account of the growth of human knowledge, in Wright's words, of "the hard-won gradual defeat of superstition and error in which we are encouraged to believe, etc., etc." Wright does not sound very sure about it; but anyhow, this is not where the real difficulty lies. The antirealist will reply that the history of knowledge, comparing hypotheses advanced at different times, must itself be given from some temporal perspective. In so doing, the scholar will be using 'true' differently from how he will use it in a year's time. He will tell the story of the past differently in a year's time. But for all this, he has a notion of diachronic inconsistency, in that he can compare the (absolute) truth values of statements made at different times. And this, he will say, is the only notion of diachronic inconsistency required to give an account of the growth of knowledge. Wright's remarks depend on his not having seen that the incommensurability move that he is criticizing already requires the distinction between the time at which a statement is made and the time at which it is being assessed for its (absolute) truth value, the distinction drawn in figures 7.1 and 7.2. Wright's own suggestion is that the antirealist can address these issues simply by double indexing: by distinguishing between the time at which a statement is made and the time at which it is being evaluated for truth or falsity. This must indeed be part of any antirealist view of the past, as we have already seen. But it is by no means a comprehensive response to the questions the antirealist faces here. For we have to acknowledge that in judging, we are always aiming at what we, at the time of judging, call 'present truth', or simply 'truth'. And then the question arises of the commensurability of our aims in judging at different times.

The real problem is, obviously, that the antirealist is in no position to recognize what I earlier called the dependent character of memory. Suppose that a year from today I remember that on this night the butler polished a revolver. The status of this memory as knowledge depends on the epistemic status of my perception today of the butler polishing a revolver. But the epistemic status of my memory judgement will relate to its being what will be called 'true' a year hence, and the epistemic status of the present perception relates to its being what we now call 'true'. And on the present account, these two goals of judgements made at different times are simply incommensurable. They are disparate, and there is nothing informative to be said about the relation between them. Consequently, the relation that ordinary thought claims to find between them cannot but be spurious. To sum up, the only way in which the antirealist can protect himself here from the charge of inconsistency over time is to appeal to the incommensurability of different temporal perspectives, but then he cannot acknowledge the dependent character of memory.

The antirealist may protest that this stepwise character of memory is simply a brute fact about the way in which we operate with memory. Once it is described, we can recognize that this is in fact the way in which we proceed, but however bizarre the practice may seem, there is no need to try to find a justification of it, and anyhow no possibility of finding one. This is simply what we do.

It needs emphasizing, though, just how peculiar this practice is on the antirealist's account. In making my judgements now I am aiming at truth, which consists in the present or future availability of evidence. In making my judgements, including memory judgements, in a year's time, I will be aiming at what I will then call 'truth', which consists in the availability of evidence then or subsequently. These are different things; evidence now available may be permanently destroyed in a year's time.

The disparity between my aim in judgement now and my aim in judgement then is wider than this, however. For on the antirealist's account, it is not the same notion of evidence that I am using now as I will be using in a year's time; there is no such generic notion of evidence. I can bring this out by remarking that in a year's time I may deny the claim that I would then express by saying that evidence was available a year ago but has since been permanently destroyed. (As we will see in the next section, this is what the antirealist presently says about the past availability of evidence.) At the moment, however, it seems entirely possible that evidence available now may be permanently destroyed in a year's time. What resolves the conflict is the incommensurability in the notions of evidence being used now and then. This incommensurability in the notions of evidence being used now and then is what underlies the incommensurability in the notions of truth being used now and then. And only the incommensurability in these notions of truth protects the antirealist from the threat of diachronic inconsistency.

In consequence of this, there is no sensible comparison to be made between the way in which I understand a concrete judgement now and the way in which I will understand it in a year's time. So it is extremely difficult to see what bearing my grounds for making the judgement now could have on the epistemic standing of the memory claims I make in a year's time. It is all very well to say: 'this is simply what we do'; but if one has given our procedures a description that makes a nonsense of them, one cannot maintain both that the description is correct and that those procedures are perfectly in order. Of course, there is no prospect of giving a justification of the stepwise conception of memory that would convince a sufficiently resolute skeptic of its correctness. But we can nonetheless ask that our procedures be described in such a way that they retain their intelligibility from within.

The fact is that we do not ordinarily experience any puzzlement about the stepwise character of memory, and this is because we have a straightforward way of rendering it intelligible. Why will my memories in a year's time depend for their epistemic status on the grounding of judgements I am making now? The reason is that both now and in a year's time, my judgements have a common goal: they aim at truth. The stepwise conception is explained by the fact that my judgements now and then have this common goal, so my memory judgement can inherit the credentials of the original judgement as a way of attaining the goal. This simple idea is what underlies the stepwise conception. The antirealist removes this stabilizer. The whole point of the position of the antirealist about the past is to deny that there is any such common goal in the formation of beliefs at different times.

7.5 Immersion

The idea that there is an incommensurability in the way in which concrete judgements are understood at different times brings the antirealist into conflict with the dependent or step-wise character of memory. But the option of incommensurability is not open for a case we have yet to consider: the relation between one's present understanding of a judgement and one's past understanding of a judgement. These cannot be taken by the antirealist to be simply incommensurable, precisely because he takes an antirealist view of the past, including his past understanding of the judgement.

Someone who opposes realism about the past insists that we are immersed in time: our present temporal perspective is not simply one among many. The idea that it is results from an attempt to interpret figure 7.2 as giving a 'sideways on' view of the relation between ourselves and reality, when no such 'sideways on' view is possible. This kind of external perspective on our own practice cannot be attained; figure 7.2 has to be interpreted from our current perspective.

Another way to put the same point is to remark that for the antirealist about the past, the notion of truth relative to the present as the time of evaluation is not simply one among a number of relativized notions. It is the primitive notion of truth that we have, and any relativized notion has to be understood in terms of it. Truth relative to a time consists in the availability, at or after that time, of evidence that can then be recognized as such. And the antirealist has an antirealist conception of the availability of evidence. For example, for the antirealist, there having been evidence for a proposition a year ago consists in there being present or future evidence that a year ago there was such evidence. There having been evidence is the same thing as its being true that there was evidence, and this is the same thing as there being present or future evidence that there was evidence (Dummett 1978, 371).

Let us now reconsider the problem of consistency in the antirealist's ascriptions of truth over time. We have seen that there are problems with the idea that these may be simply incommensurable. But this response is anyhow not available when we look at his past and present evaluations, rather than his present and future evaluations.

The problem of inconsistency in the antirealist's evaluations over time arises, as we have seen, from the possibility that evidence available at one time may be permanently destroyed. But this is a possibility that the antirealist can countenance only for evidence available now or in the future; only evidence of this sort can be permanently destroyed. For the antirealist must have an antirealist conception of the past availability of evidence. There having been evidence, on his view, just consists in the present availability of evidence that there was evidence.

Suppose now that there is past evidence for a judgement sufficient to have constituted its truth. So it receives the value true relative to that past time. This can be so only if there is present or future evidence sufficient to have constituted there having been such past evidence. But this in turn means that there is now evidence sufficient to constitute the truth of the judgement. So the judgement is also assigned the value true relative to the present as the time of evaluation. That is, it is true outright.

This move depends on supposing that evidence sufficient to constitute there having been evidence sufficient to constitute the truth of the proposition is itself evidence sufficient to constitute the truth of the proposition. Briefly, it assumes that evidence for the existence of evidence for a proposition is itself evidence for the proposition. This is one of a number of points at which the above line of reasoning might be challenged. I am not going to pursue these points here, because it seems to me that there is some intuitive force to this way of elaborating the antirealist's view, and my concern is with its consonance with our ordinary way of operating with memory.

The question is whether this approach can acknowledge the stepwise or dependent character of memory. This approach is now not appealing to an incommensurability between evaluations made at different times; on the present approach, we do not have an incommensurability between past and present evaluations. Rather, past evaluations have to be understood in terms of the present and future availability of evidence. Can this view acknowledge the dependent character of memory?

Suppose we are considering a memory that derives from a judgement based on perception, for example, my memory that the butler was wearing gloves that evening a year ago. The antirealist can now describe the stepwise conception of memory like this. For the memory impression to constitute evidence for the past-tense judgement, there must be evidence that the subject was in a position to find out how things stood otherwise than by using memory. But the memory impression itself constitutes such evidence. It is not just evidence that the thing took place; it is evidence that one was in a position to find out about it.

This does not, though, speak with precision to the point about the stepwise character of memory. In forming the original perceptual judgement about the butler a year ago, one was aiming at what one would then have called truth. One tried to adjust one's perceptual judgements to the way things were; one tried to be sensitive to the then available evidence. In forming the judgement, one could hardly have been sensitive to the then future availability of evidence, to evidence that would only become available in what was then the future. On the antirealist's account, though, whether the past state did obtain depends on the present or future availability of evidence for its having obtained. And this makes it quite impossible that one could in the past have been sensitive to whether or not the state obtained. What one took oneself to be aiming at in forming one's original judgement is quite different from what one is aiming at now in one's memory judgement.

The antirealist has no hope of securing the result that in forming one's judgements a year ago, one was managing to adjust them in the light of the present or future availability of evidence. Indeed, on his account, there having been evidence a year ago consists in the present or future availability of evidence that there was such evidence. But the antirealist can hardly claim that this was how he thought of the matter then, a year ago. He now takes it that his present perceptual judgements to have to be sensitive to the presently available evidence, rather than to the availability of evidence a year hence. And a year ago, he would have used the very same form of words to state his then current view. In his past perceptual judgements, he was not aiming at what he now calls 'truth' and cannot be represented as having been sensitive to that in his judgements.

On the approach we are considering, the truth of a past perceptual judgement is secured precisely by the present availability of evidence for it, which is provided by a memory derived from a past perceptual judgement. And in forming this past judgement, a person can hardly have been guided by whether or not he would form that memory. His forming of the past perceptual judgement was not sensitive to whether or not the subsequent memory would be formed.

The antirealist has thus still not managed to make sense of the stepwise conception of memory. For one's aim in forming the original perceptual judgement and one's aim in forming the present memory judgement remain as disparate as ever. What we would like to say is that in both cases one is aiming at truth, and that the stepwise conception is explained by the fact that both judgements have this common goal, so that the memory judgement can inherit the credentials of the original perceptual judgement as a way of attaining this goal. But the whole point of the position of the antirealist about the past is to deny that there is any such common goal in the formation of beliefs at different times.

The conflict between our ordinary use of memory and an antirealist view of the past illuminates both our understanding of memory and our understanding of antirealism about the past. It makes it evident that our practice of operating with temporal notions is deeply realist. Realism here is not simply a philosophical prejudice imposed by us on our practice; it is not simply one of the errors to which the human mind is prone. Rather, it is required by our ordinary reliance on memory. And this makes it extremely difficult to see how an antirealist view of the past can be tenable. Whenever appeal is made to some feature of our lives that conflicts with antirealism, there is a tendency for the antirealist to call it into question and to propose its revision and reconstruction. But it is difficult to see how something as fundamental as our ordinary reliance on memory could be challenged.

Notes

Chapter 1

1. See Gallistel 1990, 103 ff. For an instructive recent dispute that puts pressure on the notion of a map, see Wehner and Menzel 1990; Wehner, Bleuler, et al. 1990; and R. Menzel et al. 1990. Gallistel (1990, 123–140) gives a review of J. L. Gould's work on the map hypothesis for bees. The original paper is Tolman 1948.

2. On analyzing causation, see Salmon 1984, who uses the more general notion of a process, and for discussion, see Kitcher 1989. On objects, see Shoemaker 1984a, though his analysis is not reductive.

3. Strawson 1959, 62; see also pp. 36–38. And see Wiggins 1963 and Woods 1963.

Chapter 2

1. Gallistel 1990, 248–251. For discussions that elaborate on the distinctive features of episodic and autobiographical memory, see Nelson 1988, Nelson 1989, Rubin 1986, Tulving 1983, and Cohen 1989.

Chapter 3

1. Frege 1979, 122. I have used 'reference' where the translators have 'meaning'. See also Frege 1980, 32–34.

Chapter 4

1. I omit Meltzoff's discussion of some further refinements designed to ensure that the only salient difference between the experimenters is the content of the actions of the infant they are imitating (see Meltzoff 1990a, 145–146.

2. See also Meltzoff and Gopnik 1993. For further discussion of children's understanding of other minds, see Astington, Harris, and Olson 1988; Baron-Cohen, Tager-Flugsberg, and Cohen 1993; Gopnik 1993; Harris 1989; Perner 1991; and Whiten 1991.

Chapter 5

1. For extended discussions of this oscillation, see Nagel 1986 and Wiggins 1987.

2. This point is often held to be devastating to the reductionist's appeal to experiences. See, for example, Shoemaker 1985 and Noonan 1989, 120–121.

3. This is the position recommended to the reductionist by Shoemaker 1985.

4. McDowell 1985. Cassam (1992) pursues another parallel here.

5. For discussion of such cases, see Wilkes 1988, chap. 4.

6. An adverbial analysis of multiple personalities was proposed in lectures in Calgary by J. J. MacIntosh in 1978.

7. For defence of the multiple-occupancy thesis, see David Lewis 1983 and Noonan 1989, 164–168 and 196–198.

8. Something like this use of 'I*' is proposed by Rovane 1990, but her semantic description is sketchy, and it is not clear whether users of 'I*' also use the first person.

Chapter 6

1. For further discussion, see Frankfurt 1982, Taylor 1982, Tugendhat 1984, and Watson 1982.

2. McDowell 1976; Peacocke 1986, 86; and Wright 1987a.

Chapter 7

1. The classic statement of the problem of skepticism for a realist view of the past is Russell 1921, 159–160.

2. James 1975, chap. 15; Peirce 1934, bk. 3, chap. 4, secs. 541–545. For a brief overview of Peirce's changes of mind on the topic, see Hookway 1985, 240–246.

3. Ayer 1971, 135. Ayer later changed his view: see Ayer 1954; Ayer 1956, chap. 4; Ayer 1964, 167–168; Ayer 1968, 234–247, 310–317; and the Introduction to the second edition of Ayer 1971, 34–25.

4. This is the way in which Dummett's antirealist formulates his view. See Dummett 1978, 368.

5. See Putnam 1975a, and for an opposed view, see Sellars 1963.

6. For discussion of this view, see Stroud 1966. The view derives from Wittgenstein 1978. For a more recent discussion, see Putnam 1983.

7. The term 'cognitive dynamics' and the example come from Kaplan 1989, 537–538. For the mechanisms that underlie the ability to keep track of time, see, for example, Gallistel 1990, chap. 7.

8. So far as I know, the first appearance of this question is in Sellars 1963. Its most thorough pursuit is in Dummett 1978. There are subsequent discussions in McDowell 1978 and Wright 1987b, 1987c. None of these authors connect truth-value links to the operation of memory.

9. See McDowell 1981 for this use of the notion of externality in a different context; see also Williams 1974. For discussion of the Wittgensteinian view of the past, see Anscombe 1983.

10. See Evans 1985. Dummett has often stressed the role of truth as the aim of assertion (see, for example, Dummett 1973, chap. 10).

11. See also Foster 1985, pt. 2, secs. 1–8.

12. For the distinction, see Tulving 1983, 1984.

13. Russell clarifies his view in his later discussion of it in Russell 1984. See also Pears 1975.

14. For related remarks, see Williams 1978, 37–45.

References

Acredolo, Linda. 1990. "Behavioural Approaches to Spatial Orientation in Infancy." In *The Development and Neural Bases of Higher Cognitive Functions,* edited by Adele Diamond, vol. 608 of Annals of the New York Academy of Science. New York: New York Academy of Sciences.

Anscombe, G. E. M. 1975. "The First Person." In *Mind and Language,* edited by Samuel Guttenplan. Oxford: Oxford University Press.

Anscombe, G. E. M. 1983. "The Reality of the Past." In G. E. M. Anscombe, *Collected Philosophical Papers,* vol. 2, *Metaphysics and the Philosophy of Mind.* Cambridge: Cambridge University Press.

Astington, Janet L., Paul L. Harris, and David R. Olson, eds. 1988. *Developing Theories of Mind.* Cambridge: Cambridge University Press.

Ayer, A. J. 1954. "Statements about the Past." In A. J. Ayer, *Philosophical Essays.* London: Macmillan.

Ayer, A. J. 1956. *The Problem of Knowledge.* Harmondsworth, England: Penguin.

Ayer, A. J. 1964. *The Foundations of Empirical Knowledge.* London: Macmillan.

Ayer, A. J. 1968. *The Origins of Pragmatism.* San Francisco: Freeman, Cooper, and Co.

Ayer, A. J. 1971. *Language, Truth, and Logic.* Harmondsworth, England: Penguin.

Bairstow, P. 1986. "Postural Control." In *Motor Skill Development in Children,* edited by H. T. A. Whiting and M. G. Wade. Dordrecht, Neth.: Nijhoff.

Baron-Cohen, Simon, Helen Tager-Flusberg, and Donald J. Cohen, eds. 1993. *Understanding Other Minds: Perspectives from Autism.* Oxford: Oxford University Press.

Boyd, Richard. 1979. "Metaphor and Theory Change." In *Metaphor and Thought,* edited by Andrew Ortony. Cambridge: Cambridge University Press.

Cartwright, B. A., and T. S. Collett. 1983. "Landmark Learning in Bees: Experiments and Models." *Journal of Comparative Physiology* 151:521–543

Cassam, Quassim. 1992. "Reductionism and First-Person Thinking." In *Reduction, Explanation, and Realism,* edited by David Charles and Kathleen Lennon. Oxford: Oxford University Press.

Cohen, Gillian. 1989. *Memory in the Real World.* Hillsdale, N.J.: Erlbaum.

Cole, Jonathan. 1991. *Pride and a Daily Marathon.* London: Duckworth.

Dawkins, Marian Stamp. 1990. "From an Animal's Point of View: Motivation, Fitness, and Animal Welfare." *Behavioural and Brain Sciences* 13:1–61.

Dummett, Michael. 1973. *Frege: Philosophy of Language.* London: Duckworth.

Dummett, Michael. 1978. "The Reality of the Past." In Michael Dummett, *Truth and Other Enigmas.* London: Duckworth.

Evans, Gareth. 1985. "Does Tense Logic Rest on a Mistake?" In Gareth Evans, *Collected Papers.* Oxford: Oxford University Press.

Fodor, Jerry A. 1983. *The Modularity of Mind.* Cambridge: MIT Press.

Fodor, Jerry A. 1987. *Psychosemantics.* Cambridge: MIT Press.

Foster, John. 1985. *Ayer.* London: Routledge and Kegan Paul.

Frankfurt, Harry G. 1982. "Freedom of the Will and the Concept of a Person." In *Free Will,* edited by Gary Watson. Oxford: Oxford University Press.

Frege, Gottlob. 1952. "On Sense and Reference." In *Translations from the Philosophical Writings of Gottlob Frege,* edited by Max Black and Peter Geach. Oxford: Basil Blackwell.

Frege, Gottlob. 1967. "The Thought." In *Philosophical Logic,* edited by P. F. Strawson. Oxford: Oxford University Press.

Frege, Gottlob. 1979. "Comments on Sense and Meaning." In Gottlob Frege, *Posthumous Writings,* edited by Hans Hermes, Friedrich Kambartel, and Friedrich Kaulbach, translated by Peter Long and Roger White. Oxford: Basil Blackwell.

Frege, Gottlob. 1980. Letter to Hilbert, 1.10.1895. In Gottlob Frege, *Philosophical and Mathematical Correspondence,* edited by Gottfried Gabriel, Hans Hermes, Friedrich Kambartel, Christian Thiel, and Albert Veraart, abridged by Brian McGuinness, and translated by Hans Kvaal. Oxford: Basil Blackwell.

Friedman, Michael. 1983. *Foundations of Space-Time Theories.* Princeton: Princeton University Press.

Friedman, William J. 1990. *About Time.* Cambridge: MIT Press.

Gallistel, Charles R. 1990. *The Organization of Learning.* Cambridge: MIT Press.

Gibson, James J. 1986. *The Ecological Approach to Visual Perception.* Hillsdale, N.J.: Erlbaum.

Gopnik, Alison. 1993. "How We Know Our Minds: The Illusion of First-Person Knowledge of Intentionality." *Behavioural and Brain Sciences* 16:1–14.

Harman, Gilbert. 1986. *Change in View.* Cambridge: MIT Press.

Harris, Paul. 1989. *Children and Emotion.* Oxford: Basil Blackwell.

Hookway, Christopher. 1985. *Peirce.* London: Routledge and Kegan Paul.

Hume, David. 1888. *A Treatise of Human Nature,* edited by L. A. Selby-Bigge. Oxford: Oxford University Press.

James, William. 1975. *The Meaning of Truth.* Cambridge: Harvard University Press.

Kaplan, David. 1989. "Demonstratives." In *Themes from Kaplan,* edited by Joseph Almog, John Perry, and Howard Wettstein. Oxford: Oxford University Press.

Kitcher, Philip. 1989. "Explanatory Unification and the Causal Structure of the World." In *Scientific Explanation*, edited by Philip Kitcher and Wesley C. Salmon, vol. 13 of Minnesota Studies in the Philosophy of Science. Minneapolis: University of Minnesota Press.

Kreisel, Georg. 1969. "Mathematical Logic." In *The Philosophy of Mathematics*, edited by Jaakko Hintikka. Oxford: Oxford University Press.

Lackner, James R. 1988. "Some Proprioceptive Influences on the Perceptual Representation of Body Shape and Orientation." *Brain* 111:281–297.

Lewis, C. I. 1956. *Mind and the World Order*. New York: Dover.

Lewis, David. 1983. "Survival and Identity." In David Lewis, *Philosophical Papers*, vol. 1. Oxford: Oxford University Press.

Locke, John. 1975. *An Essay Concerning Human Understanding*, edited by Peter H. Nidditch. Oxford: Oxford University Press.

McDowell, John. 1976. "Truth-Conditions, Bivalence, and Verificationism." In *Truth and Meaning*, edited by Gareth Evans and John McDowell. Oxford: Oxford University Press.

McDowell, John. 1978. "On 'The Reality of the Past'." In *Action and Interpretation*, edited by Christopher Hookway and Philip Pettit. Cambridge: Cambridge University Press.

McDowell, John. 1981. "Non-cognitivism and Rule-Following." In *Wittgenstein: To Follow a Rule*, edited by S. Holtzman and C. Leich. London: Routledge and Kegan Paul.

McDowell, John. 1985. "Functionalism and Anomalous Monism." In *Actions and Events*, edited by Ernest LePore and Brian McLaughlin. Oxford: Basil Blackwell.

Meltzoff, Andrew. 1990a. "Foundations for Developing a Concept of Self." In *The Self in Transition*, edited by Dante Cicchetti and Marjorie Beeghly. Chicago: University of Chicago Press.

Meltzoff, Andrew. 1990b. "Towards a Developmental Cognitive Science." In *The Development and Neural Bases of Higher Cognitive Functions*, edited by Adele Diamond, vol. 608 of Annals of the New York Academy of Sciences. New York: New York Academy of Sciences.

Meltzoff, Andrew, and Alison Gopnik. 1993. "The Role of Imitation in Understanding Persons and Developing a Theory of Mind." In *Understanding Other Minds: Perspectives from Autism*, edited by Simon Baron-Cohen, Helen Tager-Flusberg, and Donald J. Cohen. Oxford: Oxford University Press.

Meltzoff, Andrew, and Keith M. Moore. 1992. "Early Imitation within a Functional Framework: The Importance of Person Identity, Movement, and Development." *Infant Behaviour and Development* 15:479–505.

Menzel, Randolf, Lars Chittka, Stefan Eichmuller, Karl Geiger, Dagmar Peitsch, and Peter Knoll. 1990. "Dominance of Celestial Cues over Landmarks Disproves Map-like Orientation in Honey Bees." *Zeitschrift für Naturforschung* 45c:723–726.

Millikan, Ruth. 1984. *Language, Thought, and Other Biological Categories*. Cambridge: MIT Press.

Millikan, Ruth. 1991. "Perceptual Content and Fregean Myth." *Mind* 100:439–459.

Müller, Martin, and Rüdiger Wehner. 1988. "Path Integration in Desert Ants, *Cataglyphis Fortis*." *Proceedings of the National Academy of Sciences, USA* 85:5287–5290.

Nabokov, Vladimir. 1980. *Lolita*. Harmondsworth, England: Penguin.

Nagel, Thomas. 1986. *The View from Nowhere*. Oxford: Oxford University Press.

Nelson, Katherine. 1988. "The Ontogeny of Memory for Real Events." In *Remembering Reconsidered*, edited by Ulric Neisser and Eugene Winograd. Cambridge: Cambridge University Press.

Nelson, Katherine. 1989. "Remembering: A Functional Developmental Perspective." In *Memory: Interdisciplinary Approaches*, edited by Paul R. Soloman, George R. Goethals, Colleen M. Kelley, and Benjamin R. Stephens. New York: Springer-Verlag.

Noonan, Harold. 1989. *Personal Identity*. London: Routledge and Kegan Paul.

Nozick, Robert. 1981. *Philosophical Explanations*. Oxford: Oxford University Press.

O'Keefe, John. 1990. "A Computational Theory of the Hippocampal Cognitive Map." In *Progress in Brain Research* 83:301–312.

O'Keefe, John. 1991. "The Hippocampal Cognitive Map and Navigational Strategies." In *Brain and Space*, edited by Jacques Paillard. Oxford: Oxford University Press.

O'Keefe, John, and Lynn Nadel. 1978. *The Hippocampus as a Cognitive Map*. Oxford: Oxford University Press.

Olton, David S. 1984. "Comparative Analysis of Episodic Memory." *Behavioural and Brain Sciences* 7:250–251.

O'Shaughnessy, Brian. 1980. *The Will*. Vol. 1. Cambridge: Cambridge University Press.

Parfit, Derek. 1984. *Reasons and Persons*. Oxford: Oxford University Press.

Peacocke, Christopher. 1986. *Thoughts: An Essay on Content*. Oxford: Basil Blackwell.

Pears, David. 1975. "Russell's Theories of Memory." In David Pears, *Questions in the Philosophy of Mind*. London: Duckworth.

Pears, David. 1984. *Motivated Irrationality*. Oxford: Oxford University Press.

Peirce, Charles S. 1934. *Collected Papers*, vol. 5, *Pragmatism and Pragmaticism*. Cambridge: Harvard University Press.

Perner, Josef. 1991. *Understanding the Representational Mind*. Cambridge: MIT Press.

Perry, John. 1972. "Can the Self Divide?" *Journal of Philosophy* 73:463–488.

Perry, John. 1979. "The Problem of the Essential Indexical." *Noûs* 13:3–21.

Pick, Herbert L., Jr., and Jeffrey J. Lockman. 1981. "From Frames of Reference to Spatial Representation." In *Spatial Representation and Behaviour across the Life Span*, edited by L. S. Liben, A. H. Patterson, and N. Newcombe. New York: Academic Press.

Poincaré, Henri. 1913. *The Foundations of Science*, transl. by G. B. Halsted. Lancaster, Pa.: Science Press.

Prince, Mortimer. 1905. *The Dissociation of a Personality*. London: Longmans.

Putnam, Hilary. 1975a. "Time and Physical Geometry." In Hilary Putnam, *Mathematics, Matter, and Method,* vol. 1 of *Collected Philosophical Papers.* Cambridge: Cambridge University Press.

Putnam, Hilary. 1975b. "Explanation and Reference." In Hilary Putnam, *Mind, Language, and Reality,* vol. 2 of *Collected Philosophical Papers.* Cambridge: Cambridge University Press.

Putnam, Hilary. 1983. "Analyticity and Apriority: Beyond Wittgenstein and Quine." In Hilary Putnam, *Realism and Reason,* vol. 3 of *Collected Philosophical Papers.* Cambridge: Cambridge University Press.

Reichenbach, Hans. 1956. *The Direction of Time.* Berkeley and Los Angeles: University of California Press.

Rousseau, Jean-Jacques. 1987. *Julie, or The New Eloise.* University Park: Pennsylvania State University Press.

Rovane, Carol. 1990. "Branching Self-Consciousness." *Philosophical Review* 99:355–395.

Rubin, David C., ed. 1986. *Autobiographical Memory.* Cambridge: Cambridge University Press.

Rubin, David C., Scott E. Wetzler, and Robert D. Nebes. 1986. "Autobiographical Memory across the Lifespan." In *Autobiographical Memory,* edited by David C. Rubin. Cambridge: Cambridge University Press.

Russell, Bertrand. 1921. *The Analysis of Mind.* London: Allen and Unwin.

Russell, Bertrand. 1967. *The Problems of Philosophy.* Oxford: Oxford University Press.

Russell, Bertrand. 1984. *The Collected Papers of Bertrand Russell,* vol. 7, *Theory of Knowledge: The 1913 Manuscript,* edited by Elizabeth Ramsden Eames and Kenneth Blackwell. London: Allen and Unwin.

Salmon, Wesley C. 1984. *Scientific Explanation and the Causal Structure of the World.* Princeton: Princeton University Press.

Scott Kelso, J. A. 1982. *Human Motor Behaviour.* Hillsdale, N.J.: Erlbaum.

Sellars, Wilfred. 1963. "Time and the World Order." In *Scientific Explanation, Space, and Time,* edited by Herbert Feigl and Grover Maxwell, vol. 3 of Minnesota Studies in the Philosophy of Science. Minneapolis: University of Minnesota Press.

Shoemaker, Sydney. 1984a. "Identity, Properties, and Causality." In Sydney Shoemaker, *Identity, Cause, and Mind*. Cambridge: Cambridge University Press.

Shoemaker, Sydney. 1984b. "Persons and Their Pasts." In Sydney Shoemaker, *Identity, Cause, and Mind*. Cambridge: Cambridge University Press.

Shoemaker, Sydney. 1985. Critical Notice of *Reasons and Persons*. *Mind* 44:443–453.

Sklar, Lawrence. 1983. "Prospects for a Causal Theory of Space-Time." In *Space, Time, and Causality*, edited by Richard Swinburne. Dordrecht, Neth.: Reidel.

Slote, Michael A. 1979. "Causality and the Concept of a 'Thing'." In *Studies in Metaphysics*, edited by Peter A. French, Theodore E. Uehling, Jr., and Howard K. Wettstein, vol. 4 of Midwest Studies in Philosophy. Minneapolis: University of Minnesota Press.

Spelke, Elizabeth S. 1988. "The Origins of Physical Knowledge." In *Thought without Language*, edited by L. Weiskrantz. Oxford: Oxford University Press.

Strawson, P. F. 1959. *Individuals*. London: Methuen.

Stroud, Barry. 1966. "Wittgenstein and Logical Necessity." In *Wittgenstein: The Philosophical Investigations*, edited by George Pitcher. London: Macmillan.

Taylor, Charles. 1982. "Responsibility for Self." In *Free Will*, edited by Gary Watson. Oxford: Oxford University Press.

Tolman, E. C. 1948. "Cognitive Maps in Rats and Men." *Psychological Review* 55:189–208.

Tugendhat, Ernst. 1984. *Self-Consciousness and Self-Determination*. Cambridge: MIT Press.

Tulving, Endel. 1983. *Elements of Episodic Memory*. Oxford: Oxford University Press.

Tulving, Endel. 1984. Précis of *Elements of Episodic Memory*. *Behavioural and Brain Sciences* 7:223–268.

Van Fraassen, Bas. 1985. *An Introduction to the Philosophy of Time and Space*. New York: Columbia University Press.

Watson, Gary. 1982. "Free Agency." In *Free Will*, edited by Gary Watson. Oxford: Oxford University Press.

Wehner, Rüdiger, S. Bleuler, C. Nievergelt, and D. Shah. 1990. "Bees Navigate by Using Vectors and Routes Rather Than Maps." *Naturwissenschaften* 77:479–482

Wehner, Rüdiger, and Randolf Menzel. 1990. "Do Insects Have Cognitive Maps?" *Annual Review of Neuroscience* 13:403–414.

Whiten, Andrew, ed. 1991. *Natural Theories of Mind*. Oxford: Basil Blackwell.

Wiggins, David. 1963. "The Individuation of Things and Places (I)." *Proceedings of the Aristotelian Society*, suppl. vol. 37: 177–216.

Wiggins, David. 1987. "The Concern to Survive." In David Wiggins, *Needs, Values, Truth*. Oxford: Basil Blackwell.

Wilkes, K. V. 1988. *Real People*. Oxford: Oxford University Press.

Wilkie, D. M., and R. Palfrey. 1987. "A Computer Simulation Model of Rats' Place Navigation in the Morris Water Maze." *Behavioural Research Methods, Instruments, and Computers* 19:400–403.

Williams, Bernard. 1974. "Wittgenstein and Idealism." In *Understanding Wittgenstein*, edited by G. Vesey, vol. 7 of the Royal Institute of Philosophy Lectures. London: Macmillan.

Williams, Bernard. 1978. *Descartes*. Harmondsworth, England: Penguin.

Wittgenstein, Ludwig. 1975. *Philosophical Remarks*. Translated by R. Hargreaves and R. White. Oxford: Blackwell.

Wittgenstein, Ludwig. 1978. *Remarks on the Foundations of Mathematics*. Oxford: Basil Blackwell.

Woods, Michael. 1963. "The Individuation of Things and Places (II)." *Proceedings of the Aristotelian Society*, suppl. vol. 37: 177–216.

Wright, Crispin. 1987a. "Anti-realism and Revisionism." In Crispin Wright, *Realism, Meaning, and Truth*. Oxford: Basil Blackwell.

Wright, Crispin. 1987b. "Realism, Truth-Value Links, Other Minds, and the Past." In Crispin Wright, *Realism, Meaning, and Truth*. Oxford: Basil Blackwell.

Wright, Crispin. 1987c. "Anti-realism, Timeless Truth, and *Nineteen Eighty-Four*." In Crispin Wright, *Realism, Meaning, and Truth*. Oxford: Basil Blackwell.

Index